MW00559282

DEEPER
BLUES

ALSO BY ANDREA SWENSSON
PUBLISHED BY THE UNIVERSITY OF MINNESOTA PRESS

Got to Be Something Here:
The Rise of the Minneapolis Sound

DEEPER BLUES

THE **LIFE,**
SONGS,
AND **SALVATION**
OF **CORNBREAD**
HARRIS

ANDREA SWENSSON
AFTERWORD BY **JIMMY JAM**

UNIVERSITY OF MINNESOTA PRESS
MINNEAPOLIS
LONDON

MINNESOTA

Published by the University of Minnesota Press
111 Third Avenue South, Suite 290
Minneapolis, MN 55401-2520
http://www.upress.umn.edu

ISBN 978-1-5179-1502-5 (hc)
ISBN 978-1-5179-1503-2 (pb)

LC record available at https://lccn.loc.gov/2024012459

Printed in the United States of America on acid-free paper

The University of Minnesota is an equal-opportunity educator and employer.

30 29 28 27 26 25 24   10 9 8 7 6 5 4 3 2 1

FOR JAMES HARRIS,
JAMES SAMUEL "CORNBREAD" HARRIS JR.,
AND JAMES SAMUEL "JIMMY JAM" HARRIS III

CONTENTS

RARE FORM

The first time I met Cornbread Harris, the Minnesota music legend had just celebrated his ninetieth birthday with a sold-out concert—and finished a short stay in the hospital that he waved away with a laugh.

Even before we officially met, there were many reasons why I was eager to speak to Cornbread. Not only was he one of the oldest musicians in the local scene to still be out performing regularly, still averaging at least a gig a week as he eased into his tenth decade, but also I knew that he had played an important role in the development of the so-called Minneapolis Sound that had long intrigued and inspired me. Way back in 1955, Cornbread had cowritten and performed on what was widely regarded to be the first rock and roll record to ever come out of Minnesota, the Augie Garcia Quintet's "Hi Ho Silver," and his live performance career extended back even earlier than that, with his first serious foray into music during World War II.

For decades, Cornbread had relentlessly pursued a music career with varying success, experiencing several brushes with almost-famousness but never quite breaking away from his status as a tireless, workman-like barroom entertainer. There was something quintessentially Minneapolis about his place in the

I

scene, I felt: even at ninety, he gigged so regularly and had been discovered and rediscovered by so many generations of hipsters and showgoers that his talents had completely been taken for granted. Yet I knew he had a hand in influencing the entire generation of musicians who get the credit for putting Minneapolis on the map in the 1980s—including his own son, James "Jimmy Jam" Harris III.

When I met Cornbread, I was working as a radio host at Minnesota Public Radio's *The Current,* and I had invited him to visit our studios to record a performance and interview that would air on both *The Current* and *MPR News* in the summer of 2017.

Cornbread entered the studio with the help of his longtime friend Chris Mozena, and the two slowly walked from the doorway over to the seat of the piano, Cornbread's back curved and shoulders slouching downward as he shuffled. Once he settled at the piano bench, however, something remarkable happened. As the studio engineer and photographer arranged cords and microphones and tripods around him, Cornbread extended his fingers over the keys and started to play. And he didn't stop the entire time he was there, not even for a second, until the whole thing was over and it was time to shuffle back out the door.

What my cohost Tom Weber and I quickly realized was that this wasn't going to be a typical session, with a preordained set list of songs punctuated by structured interview breaks. Instead, what transpired was an hour of what we would both consider to be our favorite interview we'd ever recorded, a free-flowing conversation accompanied by snippets of melodies played on the piano, occasional full performances of songs, and lots and lots of laughter.

Tom and I were theoretically the hosts for the session, but it was actually Cornbread who guided the interview with his charisma, imagination, and generous spirit. We were just along for the ride. Often, when he would interrupt a story to play something else for us on the piano, we would look at each other like two little kids who just learned they'd be having candy that day instead of lunch. It was a delight.

There were many things that surprised me about Cornbread that day, but one of the biggest was that he wore his heart on his sleeve, and that he kept everything he'd experienced, from the triumphs to the devastating setbacks, pinned onto his sleeve as well. In one short hour, and without ever deviating from his jovial, buoyant attitude, he told us about his estranged relationship with his famous son Jimmy Jam; how he'd just survived a pulmonary embolism in his lung and returned to the stage within days of receiving treatment; how he'd endured countless operations on his legs early in life and then recovered just in time to be drafted into the Army, where he first fell in love with the piano. The stories poured out, one after another, but instead of telling us about these pain points with a wince, he described them all as gifts.

"All of my hardships ended up to be blessings," Cornbread told us. "I could complain about this or complain about, 'Oh, they had to haul me off into the ambulance.' Well, that was a week ago! Shoot, later for that foolishness. I mean, this week I am here in rare form."

Another thing I learned about Cornbread, which seemed to be closely related to his relentlessly positive outlook on life, is that he became a musician because he liked pleasing people. He didn't consider himself an especially polished or accomplished musician—he was more apt to pour praise on the musicians he played with than on himself—but what kept him playing all these decades was the fact that he learned how to read charts and form enough chords that he could play pretty much any request that came his way. He told a story about how an audience member came up to him at a show once and asked him to play "Bonaparte's Retreat." After Cornbread made his way through what he felt was only a semi-accurate rendition of the tune, the man dropped a $50 bill in his tip jar. That, in Cornbread's mind, was what it was all about.

"I don't care how bad you play. If you do try to play a person's request, they appreciate it very, very much," he said. "So I don't have to be a Stravinsky or somebody, as long as I can stumble through these people's songs," he said, laughing as his eyes twinkled.

Lastly, what I learned about Cornbread that day was that despite the fact that he was known for his crowd-pleasing covers, he was also a deeply poetic and emotional songwriter. He closed the session that day with what have become my favorite two songs of his: the pleading, plaintive anthem "Put the World Back Together" and the wrenching ballad "Deeper Blues." The melodies and lyrics of those songs would stick with me for months afterward, and when I started working on this book four years later, they were some of the first things I knew I needed to ask Cornbread about.

HERE'S A FUNNY THING about life and timing: though I didn't realize it at the time, both James Samuel "Cornbread" Harris Jr. and his son, James Samuel "Jimmy Jam" Harris III, entered my life at almost the exact same time. Cornbread visited the MPR studios in July 2017, and just a few short months later Jimmy Jam returned to Minneapolis with his longtime creative partner Terry Lewis to announce a showcase they were curating to coincide with the Super Bowl happening in town that winter.

I'd wanted to talk to Jimmy and Terry for a long time. The day the three of us first chatted on the phone happened to coincide with the release of my first book, *Got to Be Something Here: The Rise of the Minneapolis Sound,* which detailed the history of a sound that they helped to make world famous. That day we talked about their earliest memories of coming up in Minneapolis, the first musicians who inspired them, and how Jimmy's mom used to take him to places like the Children's Theatre and the Walker Art Center. But one thing I noticed as we spoke, and in every interview Jimmy had done before and after that, was that he never mentioned his dad, even in passing.

For the next few years, that was all I knew about Cornbread and Jimmy: that it was complicated.

In the late spring of 2021, everything changed for the father and son—and for me. While in the midst of several of my own major life changes, I ended up getting an unexpected front-row seat to Jimmy's first attempt to reconnect with Cornbread in at least three decades. It happened when Jimmy was returning home to Minneapolis to record a segment for an awards show at Paisley Park. One day Jimmy texted me a question out of the blue: might I know how to get ahold of his dad? I gasped. I did—I could. Of course I would help. After immediately sending a few texts, I set my phone down and sighed, overwhelmed at the idea that I got to play some small bit part in a massive development in these two men's lives.

The segment that Jimmy Jam recorded for the Billboard Music Awards with his creative partner Terry Lewis and their longtime collaborators Sounds of Blackness was recorded on May 16, 2021. The next day, Jimmy went to see his dad, and the day after that he sent me a photo of the two of them together along with Jimmy's son, Max, along with a note explaining that it was the first time that Cornbread had ever met his grandson.

The following week I decided to go pay Cornbread a visit. I found him at his senior daycare facility called Augustana's Open Circle in the Near North neighborhood of Minneapolis, where he went two days a week to socialize, participate in a prayer circle, and receive light medical care. As soon as I sat down across from him, I could see that Cornbread was still glowing from his meeting with Jimmy.

"It had been twenty-four years since we had spoken to each other," Cornbread said slowly, enunciating each number and leaning toward me as he spoke. "Twenty-four years of no Jimmy. And now: Jimmy."

Suddenly it made sense why Jimmy's son, Max, who was twenty-one years old at the time, had never met his grandfather. While I would later learn that it had been much, much longer than that since Jimmy and Cornbread were in each other's lives in any meaningful way, twenty-four years was the number that had stuck in Cornbread's mind, and it was a figure he'd repeat each time we got together, as if that reunion meeting had marked the end of one era of his life and the beginning of another.

When I went to visit Cornbread that first time, we were both wearing surgical masks, and he came out to meet with me in a noisy hallway of the facility where a fountain bubbled avidly behind us, so I had to strain to hear him and struggled to project my voice so he could understand me. But we somehow found each other in the din that day, as I presented him with a copy of my book and reminded him how much I enjoyed interviewing him at the radio station. He could see I was serious, and when I nervously yelled, "Cornbread, I think I'd like to write a book about you," he let out a giddy giggle.

"Okay," he said, eyeing me and clutching the book. "Let's get to talking and make sure we understand each other. Why don't you come back next week and we'll see how things go."

And so we embarked on this new chapter of Cornbread's life

Cornbread and Jimmy Jam Harris reunited for the first time in decades at Cornbread's care facility in North Minneapolis, where Cornbread also had the opportunity to meet his grandson, Max Harris, for the first time. Courtesy of Cornbread Harris.

together, me with a recorder and pen, and him with a mind eagerly wandering from one story to the next. Every Monday for months we met in that hallway, our voices echoing off the walls and the sound of flowing water filling in the spaces between, the fountain in the lobby whirring through a cycle of endless regeneration. After a while we moved our meetings to his home where—to this day—he sits on his piano bench and presses me about information that I've found in my research while I pull out photos and newspaper clippings and ask him if he remembers this or that. Eventually our Tuesday afternoon meetings at his home became such a ritual for us both that I don't know that we'll ever stop them, even when all my research is done and the manuscript has been sent to the Press.

But I'm getting ahead of myself. Just as Cornbread did when I sat down to record our first interview all those months ago, it's best if we start at the beginning.

Chapter 1

LONG, LONG AGO

Now you are come all my grief is removed
Let me forget that so long you have roved
Let me believe that you love as you loved
Long, long ago
—"Long, Long Ago" (traditional)

"I am a blessed dude," Cornbread said, pointing a curved finger at me as he spoke. "I am a very blessed dude. That's it. You have to keep putting that in there."

Perched regally in an overstuffed armchair in the lobby of his senior care facility, Cornbread watched me closely as I wrote down each word. *Cornbread: Blessed dude.* It was a phrase he told me again and again, at least a handful of times every time we met, returning to it like a chorus as he traced the many melodies of his long life. It became, for both of us, both a mantra and an inside joke; he would often clap his hands and squeal with giggles after he said it.

James "Cornbread" Samuel Harris Jr. is a blessed dude. And that is where we will begin.

Cornbread was born on April 23, 1927, in Chicago, Illinois, to a fellow by the name of James Harris—or at least he's pretty sure that's right, if memory serves and the information that has been passed down to him is correct.

"All this stuff is talk from a different few people that I knew in the family," he said. "Am I really James Harris?" It's a big question to ask right out of the gate, but as I quickly learned, that was typical for Cornbread. He was a man who was drawn to the big questions in life—about himself, about God, about life. He loved getting lost in meandering, philosophical tangents, often cracking himself up mid-lecture and telling himself, "Okay, okay, that's enough," before finally circling back to the story he meant to tell in the first place.

It's an unusual process, getting to know someone this way. Within the first hour of our first meeting about this book, Cornbread poured his whole heart out and made sure my pen never stopped moving across my notebook pages, speaking as if it might be his one chance to have his whole life story fully heard and understood. As he reflected, it became evident that he has nurtured two seemingly contradictory, defining philosophies: that he has been dealt more than his fair share of heartache over his ninety-four years, but that despite all of it he considered everything that has happened to him to be a blessing, because it all led him to this moment when he felt lighter and happier than ever.

Our first interview came just two weeks after his son Jimmy had visited his adult daycare facility to have his first conversation with his father in decades, and Cornbread was simultaneously shocked, amazed, and eager to see where their reunion might lead.

"Twenty-four years," he told me with gravitas, emphasizing every syllable. "It had been twenty-four years since we'd spoken." He raised both hands to try to illustrate the amount of time that they had been apart, but his voice caught in his throat before he could fully explain it. "We were really separated. Really," he said, thinking about the full expanse of his life. "[In] my mind, out of the total, one end to the other, is no Jimmy. That's it. And then all of a sudden, boop, here he comes." (It would later become clear that it had actually been almost twice as long since the two had communicated in any meaningful way, likely since Cornbread and Jimmy's mother, Bertha, separated in the mid-1970s.)

Cornbread couldn't help but imagine what might happen next,

now that Jimmy was back in his life. His dream was a concert—maybe at the Hook and Ladder Theater here in Minneapolis, maybe at Carnegie Hall—where he could perform with Jimmy again. He'd even begun to draw up a set list. In order to acknowledge each of their contributions to the musical world, he hoped that Jimmy would cover two of his songs and he would cover two of Jimmy's, like a handshake between their generations.

There was only one problem: in all the hubbub around Jimmy's surprise visit to Cornbread's daycare facility, which he spent "blubbering and crying and carrying on," Cornbread later discovered he had no way to reach Jimmy, and he couldn't remember if Jimmy knew how to get ahold of him. What I would learn about Cornbread over those first few meetings is that while he had a large team of people helping him with different parts of his day-to-day life, things that I told him or notes that I gave him would often end up misplaced by the next time we met. Even when I wrote Jimmy's phone number down for him and it made it into the hands of a friend who was trying to help, they would dial it and get a strange message that the call had failed to connect.

If this all seems like a metaphor about what it's like to attempt to repair a bridge between two people that has been completely destroyed, it's because it is.

For the first several weeks that I met with Cornbread, this ache of wanting more Jimmy in his life persisted, but it wasn't our primary focus. Instead, we set out on a grand expedition through his memories, as faded and tattered as some of them may have been, to create something resembling a scaffolding of the major events of his life.

As best as he could tell, Cornbread's life story began the way all the best and most romantic stories do: with two creative, passionate people falling in love.

These are the details that Cornbread knew for sure about his early life: that he was born in Chicago, likely at Cook County Hospital, to a man who was probably named James Harris and a young woman who was definitely named Claudine King. He knew they both died tragically in his early life, by the time he was about three years old, and that he and his younger sister were raised by a series of foster parents in cities across the Midwest and then eventually by their grandparents, Thomas and Lela Wellington, in St. Paul, Minnesota.

And he was sure, beyond a shred of doubt, that his parents loved him, loved his sister, and loved each other ferociously.

When it came time to explain to me how his parents died, Cornbread took his time to spell out every detail that he knew, which he had carried with him for nearly a century.

"My dad was a gambler, a gambling man," Cornbread explained. "And it wasn't a bad gambling thing, because he was an expert gambler. One of these people they kick out of places because he could count cards, you know, and hold dice and bounce them a certain way and get the number that he wanted. . . . And so the thing that took him out was his ability to gamble that well. He was gambling in some club with a bunch of people. And he

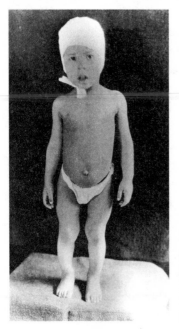

won all the money. And when the game was over, they left, and him and the bartender had a few drinks. He counted his money and put it away, tucked it away. And when he left out of there, they were waiting for him outside. They beat him up and took the money, and he died."

Oh no, I replied under my breath. "Oh yeah," Cornbread shot back, shaking his head.

When he was a toddler, Cornbread began receiving surgeries and treatments at Gillette Hospital in St. Paul to repair his legs. This photograph taken at the hospital is one of the only surviving documents of his early life. Courtesy of the Harris family.

When he told me this story, it was clear that Cornbread wanted me to know that he was proud of his father's talents, and that he was certain that he was gambling for earnest reasons. "My dad gambled. But he did it for a living!" he told me defensively, as if preemptively responding to a criticism he'd heard somewhere along the way. "He wasn't just a habitual gambler losing everything, right? He was winning. He was supporting the family."

The little information Cornbread knew about his mother was even more brief and tragic. "My mother couldn't stand that the love of her life died," he said solemnly. "So she didn't live very long after that."

The idea that someone could die of heartbreak had stayed with Cornbread all these years. It was a defining part of who he was as a person, he felt—that he came from two people who loved each other so profoundly that they literally could not live without each other. This was the basis of all the most beautiful songs that Cornbread had ever heard, and some of the finest songs that he'd written himself.

While Cornbread is most commonly described as a blues musician, his set lists have actually included dozens of genres ranging from jazz to soul to pop, gospel, big band, boogie woogie, country, Creole, and classic rock. As I got to know Cornbread's musical tastes, and as I listened to more of his recordings and live performances, I realized that the common thread between the hundreds of songs he'd learned and written was his preference for pure, pretty melodies with melancholic undertones—songs that were often hopeful and sad at the same time.

When I asked Cornbread about this, he said that's because of the great love that he was certain his parents found in each other and that he'd longed for ever since they passed.

"What I like is beautiful songs," he told me. "The melancholy comes because of the missing of closeness. That's what the melancholy is about. My mother died because they had that bond, that closeness. . . . If you're invested that deep, then you can't make it, you can't. Because this other person is such a part of you, that when that part dies, that was the part that was making you live, actually."

Months later, when Cornbread would tell me this story again at his home, he would turn around on his piano bench and play a mournful, aching rendition of Ben E. King's "Stand by Me," stopping after the first chorus to shake his head. "Oh yeah," he said, "that's dangerous."

FOR THE FIRST SEVERAL WEEKS that I went to see Cornbread, our meetings would often begin the same way. I would arrive at his adult daycare facility in the early afternoon, just as he and his friends at the center were finishing lunch. This was in the summer of 2021 and Covid restrictions were a daily concern, so I would stand in the hallway in my mask and wave through the window at the staff at the center to signal that I had arrived, then turn my attention toward setting up two armchairs next to each other in the hallway and extending a tripod to hold a recording device that I would set next to his chair.

Eventually, Cornbread would finish his lunch and one of the staff would help him stand up behind his walker, and he would do his Cornbread Shuffle out into the hall.

"Is that my book lady?" he would ask, a wry grin on his face.

"It's me," I would always reply cheerfully, doing my best to project my voice through my mask.

As soon as he settled into his armchair, he would rub his hands together eagerly and glance at my bag. "What have you got for me today?"

After going over the limited details he knew about his parents, both Cornbread and I became hungry for more—more context, more information, more of an explanation about how these two people ended up together and created such a powerful musical lineage. Together we began engaging in something resembling a call and response, not unlike the ones Cornbread had led his bands through over the past seven decades of his live performance

14

career: he would shout out a name, a city, a possible date, or a street address, and I would scribble down these valuable keywords and enter them into every newspaper and library database I could find, scanning the search results for clues.

To both of our surprise, I was able to find quite a lot thanks to the digitized newspaper archives available through the Minnesota Historical Society and services like newspaper.com. I arrived at our second interview with an entire sheath of printed pages, each one containing a newspaper clipping I'd blown up to a size he would be able to read, and he reached for the papers eagerly and read through each one slowly out loud.

Some of the first clippings we looked at together were about his mother, Claudine King Wellington. According to the Black community newspaper the *Northwestern Bulletin,* Claudine was an organist and piano teacher at her local church. This was new information for us both.

Cornbread dropped the piece of paper to his lap and looked at me in awe. "So maybe that's why I came up with this piano thing," he exclaimed. "It was in my ear, and in my heart and soul."

We kept reading. The first news item about Claudine appeared in the *Northwestern Bulletin* on April 7, 1923, when she was nineteen years old: "Miss Claudine King Wellington, 378 Jay Street, one of our young piano teachers, was selected as an organist for the C.M.E. Church by Rev. Y. J. Gamble, pastors and members of the congregation. Miss Wellington is proving to be quite successful with her pupils who are studying under her supervision."

A month later, in May 1923, an entire headline was dedicated to Claudine's new position. MISS CLAUDINE WELLINGTON ORGANIST AT GRACE CHURCH, the headline declared. The paper went on to report that "Miss Claudine Wellington is the youngest organist of our group in St. Paul. She is organist at Grace C.M.E. Church, 27 East Water Street. Why not come and hear her?"

Even more shocking to both of us was the fact that this small blurb about Cornbread's mother was accompanied by a photograph. But because of the age of the newspaper, the quality of the microfilm it had been scanned onto, and the additional warping that occurred when that microfilm was digitized and uploaded online, all that was left was a solid black rectangle that lacked any of the contours and shadows that would have brought the photograph to life.

Cornbread sighed, then picked up another paper from the stack.

In addition to clippings related to Claudine, my searches had also turned up several new clips about his grandparents, the Wellingtons, who appeared to be quite popular among the Black socialite circles of St. Paul in the 1920s. There were items about his grandmother operating a nursing, facial, and body massage business out of her home, and about his grandfather building the family a new bungalow in what is now the Como neighborhood of St. Paul. Most tellingly, there were clippings related to his mother's travels outside Minnesota to visit relatives and then to live in Chicago.

"Miss Claudine King Wellington, formerly of St. Paul, daughter of Mrs. Lela Wellington of 1144 Hand Ave., has opened a millinery shop at 3447 Vernon Ave., Chicago, Ill. She wishes any visitors from the Twin Cities to call and look

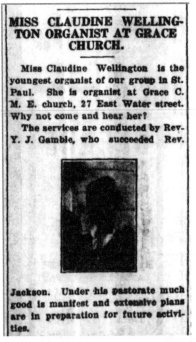

MISS CLAUDINE WELLINGTON ORGANIST AT GRACE CHURCH.

Miss Claudine Wellington is the youngest organist of our group in St. Paul. She is organist at Grace C. M. E. church, 27 East Water street. Why not come and hear her?

The services are conducted by Rev. Y. J. Gamble, who succeeded Rev.

Jackson. Under his pastorate much good is manifest and extensive plans are in preparation for future activities.

A newspaper clipping from the Black community newspaper the *Northwestern Bulletin* provided essential clues about Cornbread's mother, Claudine King Wellington. It also gave him the only photograph he had ever seen of his mother, who died when he was three years old. *Northwestern Bulletin*, May 5, 1923. Courtesy of the Minnesota Historical Society.

16

over her hats," the *Northwestern Bulletin* reported on January 31, 1925.

A year later, the *St. Paul Echo* provided an update on Claudine: "Miss Claudine King of St. Paul, the daughter of Mrs. Wellington, was married last week in Chicago. The news came as a surprise to her mother and stepfather."

"Aha!" Cornbread exclaimed, laughing at the innuendo in the article. "Good for her." The article continued: "The husband is manager of the Harris Cafe, 41st and State Sts. Mrs. Harris will discontinue her milliner business to act as secretary for her husband. Mr. and Mrs. Harris plan to visit St. Paul as soon as business will permit."

"So that's why I'm Harris," Cornbread said, sighing with relief. He did come from someone named James Harris after all.

Finding these clippings was like scanning the social media feeds of society back in the 1920s, and it was amazing just how quickly a narrative emerged about Cornbread's family. But the more I dug, the more I realized that these chestnuts existed because of how small the African American population was during this period and

---

ST. PAUL

Mrs. J. A. Gaston, 741 St. Anthony Ave., had her tonsils removed at St. Luke's Hospital, Saturday, April 17. She is now at home and getting along nicely.

Mr. and Mrs. J. A. Mitchell, are now residing at 325 N. St. Albans.

Miss Claudine King of St. Paul, the daughter of Mrs. Wellington, was married last week in Chicago. The news came as a surprise to her mother and step-father. The husband is manager of the Harris Cafe, 41st and State Sts. Mrs. Harris will discontinue her milliner business to act as secretary for her husband. Mr. and Mrs. Harris plan to visit St. Paul as soon as business will permit.

A large crowd attended the Elks' Carnival each night, given at Union Hall the past week.

A clipping from the Black newspaper the *St. Paul Echo* announced the "surprise" marriage of Cornbread's parents, Claudine King Wellington and James Harris, in Chicago. According to marriage records, they actually wed on February 27, 1926, about fourteen months before their son Jimmie was born. *St. Paul Echo*, April 24, 1926. Courtesy of the Minnesota Historical Society.

how segregated their daily life was from the white settlers that dominated the culture and news in Minnesota.

In 1920, the census found that there were only 8,809 Black people living in the entire state of Minnesota, making up 0.4 percent of the total state population. And in St. Paul, because of redlining in housing covenants and other racist city planning practices, the majority of the 3,376 Black people who were counted in the census in St. Paul lived in the vibrant Rondo neighborhood, a tight-knit "city within a city" where Cornbread's mother and grandparents lived until they moved into their new home in the almost exclusively white Como area.

Early Black newspapers like the *St. Paul Echo* and *Northwestern Bulletin* provided vital coverage of this small but blossoming community, and Cornbread and I were giddy about all that the clippings revealed. In the span of just a few short weeks and a few dozen archival searches of newspapers, birth and death records, and other vital statistics available in databases online, a story started to emerge about the people and the city from which he came.

THE YEAR WAS 1925, and the setting was the historic Bronzeville District on the South Side of Chicago, a burgeoning, sizzling hotbed of African American art, music, and culture. Known as the Black Metropolis, it became home to one of the largest Black urban populations thanks to the Great Migration, when thousands of African Americans poured into the city from across the South to flee Jim Crow–era racism and oppression. Between 1910 and 1920, the Black population of Chicago grew by 148 percent, and the Black Metropolis area population boomed to 109,548 people, creating the feeling of a smaller city nestled within a larger one, and an incubator for a generation of influential Black political, cultural, and artistic leaders.

This was an era when New Orleans expats like King Oliver were infusing Dixieland jazz into the city and passing it on to the younger players like Oliver's protégé Louis Armstrong, who became a rising star in the Bronzeville circuit in the 1920s. Venues like the Dreamland, the Sunset Cafe, and the Royal Gardens became breeding grounds for new players and new sounds, creating an ecosystem that would birth not just jazz but Chicago blues by the beginning of World War II.

One of those young Black Americans who moved northward in the early twentieth century was Cornbread's father, James Harris Sr., who migrated from his birthplace of Louisville, Kentucky, and eventually opened his own restaurant, the Harris Cafe, on the corner of 41st and State Streets in Chicago, in the heart of the Bronzeville District and just five blocks down State Street from the famous Dreamland Cafe.

Historically, Cornbread's limited information about his father certainly squared with the time and place in which he lived. In Prohibition-era Chicago, gambling had become a popular way to make (and lose) enormous amounts of money; in 1928, the *Chicago Daily Tribune* estimated there were at least 215 gambling houses in the city, including a handful within blocks of the Harris Cafe, and that an estimated $2,500,000 was played every day in underground poker, blackjack, and roulette games.

At the same time, the young musician and nursing student Claudine King Wellington was coming of age in St. Paul, Minnesota, and dreamed of moving to a bigger city to pursue her own path. Claudine was already used to moving around; by the time she reached adulthood, she had already lived with her family in Denver, El Paso, Bemidji, and St. Paul. She ventured out on her own to start a new life on the South Side of Chicago when she was just twenty years old.

James and Claudine married on February 27, 1926, and it's possible that Claudine waited a few weeks to tell her mother and stepfather back home, as her hometown paper wouldn't report on their "surprising" nuptials until April. By the summer's end, she would be pregnant with her first child, whom they would name Jimmie Samuel Harris Jr. when he was born on April 23, 1927.

Another child soon followed, and James and Claudine came to St. Paul for the birth of Veola Marcelline Harris in November 1928. On Veola's birth certificate, the address for both James and Claudine was listed as 1144 Hand Avenue, the home of the Wellingtons. It's possible that the young Harris family came to St. Paul so that Cornbread, then known as little Jimmie, could be treated at Gillette Hospital; a photo of him was taken there around this time. But at this point in the story, there are no other public records to illuminate the family story. All Cornbread knew was that by the time he was about three, both of his parents were gone.

"I was born a throwaway baby," Cornbread told me bluntly, scanning my eyes for a reaction. It was a jarring statement, and it caught me off guard every time he said it, even after we'd been meeting for months. "I was born bowlegged and pigeon-toed. And I use the phrase, and people get shocked. But I was a throwaway baby."

Cornbread said he began receiving medical treatments for the disabilities in his legs when he was just a toddler, likely when his parents were still alive and continuing for years as he was shuffled around to several foster homes with his younger sister. By his estimation, Cornbread spent the first seven or eight years of his life in and out of hospitals, enduring countless surgeries, casts, and braces until he could finally walk on his own.

"God got the people together," he explained. "They started breaking my legs and putting them in casts and then breaking them, putting them in casts again. And then therapy, therapy, and therapy. Man, when I could finally walk, no cane, no wheelchair, no walker, no nothing? I couldn't figure out how come people couldn't appreciate the fact that they can walk. What a blessing it is. And so I just have an appreciation for things. Man, I am such a blessed dude. I'm a blessed dude."

To illustrate his point, Cornbread stood up suddenly from his chair and grabbed a hold of his walker, then took off speed-walking down the hallway, almost breaking into a jog. It was quite a sight, seeing a ninety-four-year-old man suddenly get up and start running, but that's how eager he was to prove that his legs were still strong. When he got back to his chair, he laughed and shoved his walker out of the way, walking the last few steps alone.

"Top speed!" he said proudly. "That's what they call in-de-pen-dent."

Although Cornbread spent two days a week at his adult day-care facility, where he enjoyed fraternizing with other elderly patients, teasing the staff, and receiving hot meals and routine medical care, he still spent most of his time living independently at home with his wife, Sabreen Hasan. We began meeting at the day-care facility because it was a comfortable space for him to receive guests, but before long he started suggesting that he wanted me to visit him at home instead, where he could have easy access to his journals and scrapbooks, and where he could regale me from the bench of his beloved piano. We would get there eventually. For now, he got a kick out of showing me how quickly he could cruise up and down the halls of the daycare center.

Once he settled down, he returned to telling me about his early life. Cornbread didn't remember much about where he was living when he was receiving the treatments on his legs, or the families that he and his sister Veola stayed with during the years they were in foster care. The two young orphans were bounced around quite a lot—Cornbread remembers them living first in Omaha, then Detroit, St. Louis, and Denver, before ending up in St. Paul. He guesses that the adoption agency had some kind of time limit on how long they could stay with each family before they had to decide whether he and his sister would be adopted, which caused them to move around so much.

"I lived in all kind of different homes. Some I liked, some I didn't like," he recalled. "This one I couldn't stand. The fella used to sit in the kitchen and eat lutefisk. Oh, yeah. It'd smell up the whole house. I couldn't stand that house. And he was just as comfortable as he could be."

Cornbread remembered that once he and Veola got to St. Paul, they were staying with a family who lived on St. Anthony Avenue in the Rondo neighborhood. "And the lady knew my grandparents," he explained. "So that's how I ended up getting back with the grandparents."

By the time Cornbread was eleven, he was living with his grandparents Thomas and Lela Wellington in the Como neighborhood of St. Paul, and he and Veola were enrolled at the almost exclusively white Catholic school St. Bernard's. He had finally found something resembling a stable home life, and his time at St. Bernard's opened his eyes to many larger concepts he hadn't fully considered before, including religion, music, and racial discrimination.

"I lived at 1144 Hand Avenue, on the corner," Cornbread recalled, "and Geranium was the street I walked to go to school. At St. Bernard's School, where I got my fingers swatted, where I got baptized a Catholic and started my catechism, and oh, I never got a chance to forget I was Negro. I got beat up quite a bit at school, in the playground. And so I was trying to just fend it off, you know, and not get into any trouble with it, and I ended up having to beat the guy up. And he let up off of me then. And I didn't feel good beating him up. I didn't feel good about that. But it worked. So then that brought my reputation up to where they left me alone."

Cornbread said that he and his grandparents ended up in such a predominantly white area (something that was especially rare for Black people in Minneapolis and St. Paul, where racist housing covenants restricted people of color from buying property outside designated areas) because his grandfather, Thomas Wellington, passed as white. "My grandfather was mulatto, so he looked like a white man," Cornbread explained. "He got a good job on the railroad as a conductor. He wasn't a waiter or a porter, which the Negroes were very in monopoly on those two jobs. But the job he had, there was no Negroes. So when he built the house at 1144 Hand, he came and bought the house; there was

A young Jimmie Harris, age eleven, was photographed with his fifth grade class at St. Bernard's School on St. Paul's North End. The Catholic school was located a few blocks from his grandparents' home. Courtesy of the St. Bernard's Archives.

Jimmie Harris and his younger sister, Veola, were among the only students of color at the predominantly white Catholic school. Courtesy of the St. Bernard's Archives.

no problem there. But then he sent for his wife after he got the house, and she was Negro and looked Negro. And the people wanted to figure out how come this Negro lady was goin' in this white man's house. And the trouble started, with mischievous things being done to the house and stuff like that."

According to the *Northwestern Bulletin,* the Wellingtons had their home on Hand Avenue built in 1924, shortly after Cornbread's mother Claudine departed for Chicago. The newspaper described it as "a beautiful bungalow on the corner of Hand and Geranium streets. The home will be strictly modern, with the latest built-in features, and was designed by his [Thomas's] wife, Mrs. Lela Wellington." Cornbread and his sister wouldn't end up living there until 1938, but the discrimination they were experiencing as the only Black family on the block endured.

"And of course, since I was coming out of foster homes and stuff, I was paying attention to my surroundings," Cornbread said. "Yeah, definitely paid attention, and paid attention to how people acted. What people said, and did it match what they did? I remember telling my sister, I said, 'You know what, these fellas are going to try to take you down. You're a pretty girl.' I had a pretty long talk with her, like a daddy sits down with a child."

It's a lot for an eleven-year-old kid to take on, but given how much Cornbread and his sister had been through by this point, he said he took it all in stride. Looking back on it several decades later, he mainly recalled this period of his life fondly, as his time attending St. Bernard's and living on Hand Avenue (now called Virginia Street) allowed him to explore his first hobbies and passions, including sports and music.

"I was trying to get away from music," Cornbread recalled, laughing. "I was trying to be in sports, because, like I said, being bowlegged and pigeon-toed, couldn't walk, couldn't run. I wanted to be an athlete. But God gave me the music talent. And I didn't want to do that. My grandparents wanted me to be educated, sophisticated. So they figured music was a good thing that I should have. But when my friends would come by talking about,

'Could Jimmie come out and play?' And then my grandparents are talking about, 'No, he can't, he got to practice.' I mean, come on," he said, shaking his head.

One of the stories Cornbread loved to tell about this period was how he devised a plan to skip his piano lessons with the knuckle-swatting nuns at St. Bernard's and keep the money to buy treats for himself instead. "The way they found out was the teacher called up the house. 'Where's Jimmie?' 'He's in music lessons.' 'No, he isn't. I'm the teacher and he's not here.' And I'd spent the money, bought candy, you know, bananas, apples, whatever. And would give it out to my friends and hang out in the school playgrounds, which was just, you know, a block away. I got away with it for a month, month and a half. Until that call, you know."

"And then they didn't come down on me right away," he continued. "My grandma gave me the money after she already knew. Says, you know, 'Okay, it's time for you to go to music lessons. By the way, how come you keep playing that same song over and over all the time?' I said, 'They're really strict. I can't get a new song until, you know, I get this one perfect.' I thought that would cover it. I got away with it a couple of times. And then she told me the second or third time, 'I'm gonna tell your dad.' They didn't call themselves grandparents. 'I'm going to tell your dad,' and I said, 'Oh boy, I'm in trouble now.' Because he was the disciplinarian of the family. So he got the news. He came to talk to me. I said, 'Uh oh, here we go.' He said, 'Go down in the basement.' Because that was his deal. He went into the bathroom and got the razor strip and wore my little behind out. So anyway, that was the end of my music lessons. I didn't get to go no more and spend that money."

As he told the story, Cornbread's eyes twinkled, like he was still impressed that he had gotten away with his lesson-skipping gimmick for as long as he did. Though it was a bumpy start to his music career, he did come away learning one song, the traditional "Long, Long Ago," which was originally written in 1833 by the English composer Thomas Haynes Bayly but had been revived during Cornbread's childhood by popular artists of the era like Glenn Miller.

At just the mention of the title, Cornbread breaks into song, humming the whole melody aloud. "I will remember that song the longest day that I live," he said. "I think I might forget everything else, but I'm sure I'll remember that tune."

I DIDN'T KNOW HOW MUCH TIME I would have with Cornbread. I wasn't sure how long he'd have the patience to sit and reminisce with me, or how long his memory would hold out. At that point, I certainly had no idea that we'd spend three years (and counting) getting together every week, first every Monday afternoon at his daycare facility and then every Tuesday at his home off Olson Memorial Highway in North Minneapolis.

Even as our time together stretched on and we grew closer, though, every moment with him felt like it might be our only chance to piece together his fragmented past. I wanted so badly for him to experience and rediscover as much of his life as he could.

That summer of 2021, as we got to know each other and unfolded his story together, I couldn't stop thinking about that blurred, blacked-out photograph of his mother from the St. Paul newspaper archives. What would it mean for Cornbread if he had the opportunity to see his mother's face? Would he remember what she looked like? Would it help him to find peace in this tragic story that he told and retold about his early life?

As the summer wound down I decided to go to the Minnesota Historical Society to see if I could view the newspaper. The History Center had just reopened its library and microfilm room to researchers after being locked down because of Covid, and it had been several years since I'd worked a microfilm machine, so I asked a librarian for help—and as soon as I started trying to explain what I was doing, I felt my voice catch in my throat.

"I'm trying to find a clipping for my friend," I explained. "His mother was photographed for this newspaper back in 1923. She died a few years later, and he's never even seen a picture of her."

"We are going to get this in focus," the librarian said, determined to join me on my mission.

Together we hunched over the microfilm machine and watched as the reel of film unspooled over the glass and whirred by on the screen above. Eventually she stopped the reel and gently eased it on the right page, then zoomed in on the article announcing Claudine King Wellington and her new role playing organ at the local church.

"That's her!" I said. The photograph didn't look much better in person, but the librarian slowly turned the dials of the machine until the words of the article had all but faded away. As she lightened the image, an outline of a young woman's face began to appear. She had a high white collar pulled up around her neck and her hair swooped over the left side of her face and then back into a bun, and she smiled politely toward the camera, her cheekbones high and pronounced, a warm presence emanating from the blurry, century-old photograph.

She looked like Jimmy Jam.

I thanked the librarian profusely, printed out the image, took a few photos of the screen with my camera, and headed home. I couldn't wait to show Cornbread.

A few days later, I called Cornbread to remind him that I was on my way over. I could barely contain my excitement. "I have something to show you," I said.

"Oh good! Bye-bye for now, God bless," Cornbread said, hanging up the phone.

As soon as we were settled into our chairs, I pulled out a folder and tried to explain to Cornbread what I'd found. "Do you remember my telling you I found an article about your mother in the paper?"

"Something about my mother?" he said, sounding surprised.

"And how she was an organist at the church? So they had this article about her, and the picture was really hard to make out.

But I went and found the newspaper on microfilm. And I tried to get it as clear as I could. And I think you can see a little bit—I blew it up really big."

"That's my mother?" he asked, raising his eyebrows at me. "1923—and four, five, six, seven—four years later I was born."

"Yeah!" I confirmed.

"Man, I had a pretty mama!" he exclaimed, bringing the sheet of paper up to his face. "Well, as good as I can see, that picture looks perfect," he said, giggling. "Man. Oh man. Oh Lord. How do I get people to do for me like this? I don't have the slightest idea. My mother. My mother."

As he stared at the photograph, the familiar story of heartache came rushing back. "She married this dude that was a gambler. And he got killed in a gambling game. And she loved him so much. She lived only maybe a year after that. Oh man. I'm glad she didn't die before she had me."

"Had you seen pictures of her before?" I asked.

"No, no. I don't have any pictures," he said. "Oh wow. I'm going to actually know the story of who I am, pretty soon."

"That's the plan!"

"Is that what the plan is? Because I just swore that since I had all this interest in outer space, somebody just came and dropped me down here like Superman. But I didn't have any superpowers or nothing, so I don't know," he said. "But I probably do have superpowers, and I think that's what sustained me through all of that. And of course, that brings me to God, blessing me from the day I was born by this lady, and taking care of me ever since then. That was ninety-four years ago. Oh Lord. I mean, how do you cover ninety-four years?"

"We'll do it one week at a time," I replied.

"Yeah," he said. "Oh, yeah."

Chapter 2

HEART AND SOUL

Heart and soul, I fell in love with you
Heart and soul, the way a fool would do, madly
— "Heart and Soul," Frank Loesser and Hoagy Carmichael

A fter two months of our getting together every Monday afternoon at his daycare facility, Cornbread decided that it
was time for us to move our interview sessions to his home, where
he could be in closer proximity to his memorabilia and, most cru-
cially, to his piano. Cornbread and his wife lived on a quiet resi-
dential street just two blocks north of Olson Memorial Highway
in North Minneapolis, a stretch of road that was once home to
dozens of small family-owned businesses and now slices through
the area like a miniature freeway. His house was a stone's throw
away from where Prince's father once lived and where other musicians of Prince's generation like Morris Day, André "Cymone"
Anderson, and Terry Lewis all came of age.

Most important to Cornbread, his house was just a block up
from the historic Zion Baptist Church, which played a foundational role in fortifying the Black community in North Minneapolis and where Cornbread still attends church every Sunday.

I pulled up to a modest yellow two-story house with a beautiful garden filling every inch of the sloped front yard. As soon
as I climbed the steps and set foot on the front porch, a motion detector set off a screeching alarm that alerted those inside

29

Cornbread bids me adieu after one of our Tuesday afternoon meetings at his home in North Minneapolis. Courtesy of the author.

to my presence. Before long, the front door swung open, and I was greeted by Cornbread's wife, Sabreen Hasan, and youngest daughter Jennifer Harris: both intended to scope me out before leaving me alone to talk to Cornbread.

Once inside, it became clear that Cornbread spent most of his time shuffling between two rooms on the first floor of his home: his bedroom, which sat just inside the front door and included a small bed and a desk where he logged phone calls and kept track of his gigs, and the dining room where he kept his well-loved and weathered upright piano. A small hallway joined his bedroom to the kitchen and dining room and was lined with photographs and awards, and Cornbread was eager to show me how he had nearly run out of wall space on which to hang his lifetime of accolades.

As we settled into the dining room, Cornbread and I assumed positions that we would return to every week for months, then years to come. He would slowly plod in and sit down at his piano bench, facing into the room, and I would tuck myself into the seat of an old diner booth right across from him. Within the first five minutes of our first interview in this space, Cornbread recognized the benefit of this arrangement: anytime he got tired of talking or just wanted to explain something musically rather than verbally, he could slowly swivel around on his bench and place his hands on the old ivory keys.

"Oh, you've never been around me when I had one of these," Cornbread said excitedly, understanding that the piano could now play a role in our conversations. As he slowly, methodically swiveled around to face the keys, he said, "This is my 'Blue Blue Blue Blues.' This is my opening song on every gig." Cornbread felt his way around the keyboard, warming with a couple of impressionistic chords and stabs of notes, then eased into a blues scale and a steady chord progression. The more he played, the more tender and nuanced the song became, as his right hand felt out improvised melodies and his left hand settled into a familiar walking bass line.

I don't know if you've ever had the chance to sit a few feet away from someone who has been playing an instrument for the better part of nine decades, but it never got old for me, even when I'd seen him play hundreds of times. There was something simply wondrous about watching Cornbread's hands come to life over those keys; while he made it look effortless, I know that the graceful way that his fingers navigated scales and licks was the result of untold hours of practice and playing. Cornbread had a light touch, and once he really settled into a song it was easy to get lost in his playing with him, as if we were both suspended in a daydream.

Once he finished this particular song on this particular day, he told me the title again, making sure that I picked up my pen and wrote it down. "That's my 'Blue Blue Blue Blues,' and it's never the same way twice. That's my thing. That's me," he said, thumping his pointer finger against his chest. "You saw me. You heard me."

Cornbread regarded "Blue Blue Blue Blues" as his theme song and his calling card, and in our time together he would continuously rework and reimagine the way he wanted his band to help him kick off the song. Though there was a familiar refrain that always appeared at the beginning of the number, he was correct to say that he never played it the same way twice; sometimes he would play it for me for only thirty seconds, and sometimes his performance could stretch for ten minutes or more.

Years from now when I look back on this treasured time I spent with Cornbread, I think this image will forever be blazed into my brain: a ninety-four-year-old man resting his weathered hands over his piano keys and floating away, his shoulders hunched and head bent in quiet reverie. Each time he played, it seemed like Cornbread was transported back to being a young man again, still in awe of what he could create on this instrument that had occupied so much of his time for so many years.

It's a cliché to say that music is healing, but as I spent more time with Cornbread I became convinced of its powers. The playing, the performing, the connectivity that he found in this liminal space between his creative subconsciousness and his waking life—I am certain that the piano is what kept all his other faculties so sharp, what kept him going through Covid lockdowns and isolation, and what kept Cornbread alive well into his tenth decade.

As he loved to tell me again and again, Cornbread's entrance into music—with the knuckle-cracking nuns and his ill-fated scheme to skip his piano lessons—did little to predict the lifetime of joy that he would eventually pursue with this instrument. But even though he tried to avoid it, music played a recurring role in his early life and helped to lay a foundation for what was to come.

Decades before he would become known as Cornbread, the young Jimmie (sometimes spelled Jimmy) Harris Jr. had finally settled into a more stable, peaceful home life while living with his grandparents in St. Paul. As a preteen and teen, this was an era when his attention turned toward playing sports, keeping his teachers on their toes at school, and buying his first recorded music. Coming of age in a predominantly white neighborhood meant that some of his earliest musical interests were the popular country stars of the late '30s and early '40s.

"Man, Roy Rogers and all of them, they were my idols, you know?" Cornbread remembered. His first records were by 1940s country stars like Gene Autry, Hank Williams, and Minnie Pearl, and those influences ended up merging with the big band sounds of the day by artists like Benny Goodman, Duke Ellington, and Count Basie and the spiritual music he heard in the Black church to inform his earliest sense of rhythm and melody.

Once he was old enough to venture out on his own as a teenager and explore the Rondo area, he said the historic Black neighborhood provided him with his first introduction to the blues. He still remembered hearing B. B. King for the first time like it was yesterday. "Once I got a hold of the blues, then I said, 'Oh my goodness.' I started playing blues no matter what the song was,"

Cornbread remembered, laughing. "And once that happened, it was liked really well, and it wasn't like anybody else played them, so I was original with the way I played a song."

What's fascinating is that Cornbread didn't have many memories of playing music as a teenager; the way he recalled it, he didn't reconnect with the piano and uncover his talent for it until he was enlisted in the Army. But as I turned up more and more newspaper clippings about his early life, we both learned together that Cornbread was something of a star pupil in the early 1940s.

While combing through hundreds of clippings that spanned his entire life and career, I came across what is likely Cornbread's first mention in a local paper: a celebration of his thirteenth birthday hosted by his grandmother Lela Wellington on April 23, 1940, which was mentioned in the *St. Paul Recorder*. His momentous birthday party happened the same year that he was preparing to finish at St. Bernard's Catholic school and enter high school, first at Washington High School and later at Mechanic Arts High School in downtown St. Paul, and around this same time he became more involved in the Black church. By 1942, when he turned fifteen years old, Jimmy Harris Jr. was making the paper for his standout roles acting in plays and performing in piano recitals at Welcome Hall, a Black community center adjacent to Zion Presbyterian Church in Rondo.

"The monthly recital given by the pupils of Mary Short, Friday, March 27, was well attended and showed much advancement in the pupils presented," one clipping read. "Mrs. Short gave three tickets for the Philippa Duke Schuyler Recital to the pupils doing the most outstanding work. The winners were Marion Williams, Harry Estees and James Harris."

"Whoa, wow! I was a winner!" Cornbread exclaimed. "Whoa, man. I was on the road early. Fifteen years old? Wow."

Another surprise came when I went digging for Cornbread's old school yearbooks. In 1944, when Cornbread was a junior at Mechanic Arts, he joined the school's new marching band program and took up the tuba. He was photographed along with the

'There Is Music In The Air'

Row 1—K. Wilkus, L. Reimer, A. Chapin, V. Robinson, C. McWatt, A. Juds, R. Stolaas, B. Jensen. Row 2—C. Fourt, M. Steinman, B. Callon, T. McDonald, A. Watson, E. Kuehn, M. Lindemann. Row 3—J. Harris, G. Oler, M. Thompson, S. Dufour, G. Paul, L. Powers, H. Lasman, D. Lorentson. Row 4—G. Harris, S. Nordby, B. Kaplan, J. Tester, S. Dresser, P. Kendrick, A. Stella, J. Kawakami.

A photograph from the Mechanic Arts High School yearbook that helped to remind Cornbread that he played the tuba in the school band—an experience that still informed his boogie-woogie bass-driven piano playing decades later. *M,* St. Paul, 1944. Courtesy of the Minnesota Historical Society.

rest of the band, holding a tuba and looking stoically toward the camera.

"So this is why I've always loved the tuba," Cornbread exclaimed. "Because I could actually play one, at one time! Oh, Lord. I played the tuba."

I handed Cornbread a photocopy of the yearbook page, and he held it close to his face, reading over the names of his old classmates and the captions beside the photos. Though he didn't have any clear memories of his time as a tuba player, it appeared he was part of a growing music program at Mechanic Arts that

35

introduced dozens of his classmates to new instruments. "Although the band started in September with only six members from last year, it grew by March to an enrollment of 40," the yearbook explained.

"Well, I'll be sideways," Cornbread said, dropping the paper to his lap.

By the next week, Cornbread was starting to piece together how his time playing the tuba in high school might have informed his playing later on in life. "I remember now, how come I like that running bass," he told me the next time I visited. "I played tuba!"

"That's right," I said.

"When I was young," he continued, "and my ear for bass, that bass line—" He cut himself off midsentence and started humming a walking blues bass line, then turned to his keyboard to illustrate what he meant. "I never could just block the bottom two notes and play a chord." He broke into a short blues improvisation on the piano, with his left hand working out a bouncing bass line while his right hand played a slinky melody.

"So it all goes back to the tuba," I noted.

"Yeah, back to the tuba, baby!" he said, grinning.

Even when he was still in high school, the teenaged Jimmy Harris Jr. had plans to join the service and help the American forces overseas in World War II. He remembered attending at least three different high schools, including Washington, Mechanic Arts, and Cretin High School, which was more explicitly geared toward preparing young men to join the military.

According to his Army records, Cornbread earned his high school diploma in 1945 and enrolled in a year of liberal arts studies at the University of Minnesota that fall, where he studied American and world history, biology, and solid geometry. While in his first year at the university, however, he enlisted in the United States Army and entered active service on May 9, 1946, when he had just turned nineteen.

Looking back at his time in the service, Cornbread had mixed feelings. On the one hand, he was proud of what he accomplished

A World War II draft card shows Cornbread's home address and place of employment at the time he enlisted in the Army. A typo caused his grandmother Lela Wellington's name to be misprinted as Lena. Courtesy of Cornbread Harris.

during his year of training at Fort McClellan in Alabama, where he worked as a military policeman and earned high scores as an expert rifleman. But because of the timing of his enlistment, which happened in the immediate aftermath of World War II and just before the start of the Korean War in 1950, his time in the Army never extended beyond the training base and, considering all the gruesome injuries and deaths sustained by other soldiers of his generation, he still carried something resembling survivor's guilt about it well into old age. Cornbread said that he remembered watching as each draft rolled around and feeling a swirl of complicated emotions every time his name wasn't pulled out of the barrel. Eventually, he became a truck driver on the Army base and drove to pick up soldiers who were returning from overseas.

"Guys were coming home on the train, and they rode in the back of the truck like cattle," he remembered. "And the stories I heard about those guys going through that thing, with their

James Samuel Harris enlisted in the Army and entered active service on May 9, 1946, when he was nineteen years old. Courtesy of the Harris family.

friends being blown up? I mean, it's no wonder they'd come back with that syndrome, PTSD. It's no wonder. People come back from there with plates in their head, arms and legs gone, and minds just completely washed away. I kept thinking, man, I could have been one of these people."

As he observed the casualties of war and prepared for his own turn to head to battle, Cornbread found a bright spot while spending downtime with injured troops—where the base happened to have a piano. "I played music in the dayroom for the soldiers," he remembered, then turned to his piano to play a couple of the rudimentary songs that he knew by heart at that time. They included the one that every kid somehow learns, which involves thrumming your knuckles across the black keys and pounding a fist on either end of the octave; another childhood classic, "Heart and Soul"; and, of course, "Chopsticks."

"And they said, 'Oh, my goodness, you play the piano!'" Cornbread remembered, laughing at how fun it was to entertain the troops with his modest abilities. "I couldn't play none of the songs well."

In an interview he gave back in 2002 with the Loring Park community paper *One Nation News,* Cornbread expanded on the songs he played for the troops in the dayroom—a space he came to enjoy, because it was where everyone went to feel relaxed. "'Long, Long Ago' was a hit," he said, referring to the first song he ever learned on the piano. "'In the Mood' was a bigger hit. That was a song people knew and liked." In a separate interview, he also recalled fumbling through "Boogie Woogie Bugle Boy," a hit from fellow Minnesotans the Andrews Sisters.

When I read these old clippings to Cornbread, he became even more animated about the reactions he received to his uncertain performances. "They just loved my four songs!" he exclaimed. "And that was it—I couldn't play nothing else. I didn't have no idea how I could. But they had all been burned by a memory of action more than music," he said, miming the action of hammering away on his piano keys. "So I had them actions together, you know, and I would have to play them songs over and over for those guys. That's when I got it into my brain: people love music."

Even when he was decades into his career, Cornbread still approached his piano playing the same way, like it was an act of service and an opportunity to spread joy and light to people as they navigated an often cruel world. Without ever stepping foot on a battlefield, Cornbread's time in the Army shaped him into the man he would become and laid out a path that he would walk for the rest of his life.

Cornbread was honorably discharged from the Army on June 8, 1947, when he was twenty years old. As soon as he returned to the Twin Cities, several major life events were set into motion: he met his first serious love interest, Dollie Schuck, and got married; he welcomed his first daughter, Cynthia; and he formed his first real band, the Swing Masters, which would perform off and on for the next fifteen years.

"I got married as soon as I came out of the Army," he said. He remembered meeting Dollie and her entire family while visiting friends on Emerson Avenue in North Minneapolis that summer after returning home. "I was still wearing my uniform, and that's what won them all over," he recalled, chuckling. "And Dollie kept on needling me and treating me nice and everything, so I said, 'Well, okay!'"

The birth of his daughter Cynthia was a watershed moment in his life. The father and daughter remained close for decades, until Cynthia's untimely death from cancer in 2005 at the age of fifty-five. "She was just the most wonderfulest, kindest, sweetest daughter," he said, sighing.

NOT MANY OTHER MEMORIES REMAINED for Cornbread of this part of his early adult life. In fragments, and depending on the day, he recalled various odd jobs he strung together to make a living in those early post-military years: driving cabs, cleaning houses in South Minneapolis, even touring with the local carnival circuit to set up and operate a Ferris wheel.

He supported this work with gigs as the bandleader of the Swing Masters, a revolving big band group that he formed with an old classmate, Ron Finney, when he was twenty-one years old. "They had this old raggedy piano on the porch, which wasn't heated or nothin', and we'd sit out there and practice," Cornbread told *One Nation News* in 2002. "I was playing chitlin struts—rent parties, backyard parties, weddings, whatever."

Looking back on the Swing Masters in his nineties, Cornbread mostly recalled how loose and improvisational the group became, and how closely the ethos of the band ended up mirroring his work as a bandleader in his later years, when he would welcome a rotating cast of local players to sit in with him and jam at Palmer's Bar.

"That's where I got my experience that I'm using at Palmer's," he explained. "I could see these bands, right? They've got the stands, they've got this director guy, they've got the music sitting on there, and everybody's playing a part. And I didn't have all that. We played just off your head, off of what you heard, and then somebody else would hear you and they would echo, and do a call-and-response. It was just like today: 'What song are you going to play? Do you know it? Well, listen.' It's a communication, like talking—you learn the language."

The first mention of the Swing Masters in the *St. Paul Recorder* appeared in February 1953, when Cornbread and his band were playing at a young woman's surprise birthday party in Rondo. "Dancing was the feature of the evening," the account in the paper read. "Music was furnished by a four piece orchestra, James Harris and his Swing Masters. Cocktails were served followed by a delicious shrimp supper."

"Yeah! Oh man, there it is, there it is," Cornbread said when I read him the clipping. "I remembered Swing Masters as this thrown-together thing, but here I'm already an established group." He laughed and clapped his hands. Cornbread recalled that he would have been living in Rondo by this time as well; he purchased his first house for his young family at 898 Carroll Avenue, an address he could still recite proudly decades later.

Although this was a time of exciting new beginnings for him, it was also a period of his life marked by another tragedy: in the summer of 1950, Cornbread's grandparents, Thomas and Lela Wellington, were involved in a serious car accident while driving through Iowa. Thomas died two weeks after the accident, and Lela was seriously injured and moved to a rest home, where she died on March 19, 1951.

"My grandparents had a Pierce Arrow, a fine car, big, boxy thing," Cornbread recalled. "I admired that car so much that I used to come out of the house and stand on the landing and look at the car, just stand there and look at it. One day I looked out there, the car was gone. What happened to the car? Next thing I knew, there was a brand-new Nash Rambler in the garage. And I thought, why did they do that? They had a beautiful car, and now they got one of these cheap, brand-new type cars. And so they had the car for five or six months, and they decided to go on vacation. And they went out and crashed that car."

Cornbread and his younger sister, Veola, were each new parents at this time, and much to their surprise they were given ownership of their grandparents' home in Como, where they had spent their formative years coming of age. "They had made provisions for me and my sister to have that house," Cornbread recalled. "Then the lawyer came—he couldn't believe it. That was our house. Oh man, when I say I'm a blessed dude," he says, shaking his head and returning to his life's chorus, "when I start remembering all of the things, regardless of all the bad things that happened, all the wonderful things that happened—I've been blessed and blessed and blessed and blessed."

The Harris siblings sold the house and split the proceeds, allowing Veola to move to Denver and open her own café, and Cornbread to buy his first home in Rondo. Around that same time, he got a steady job working at the foundry American Hoist and Derrick, just south of downtown St. Paul. He would work there for decades, and the job provided some stability to a life that was about to endure more highs and lows.

By the end of the 1950s, Cornbread would experience the dissolution of his first marriage and the rebuilding of a new relationship and home life, and he would welcome his second child, James Samuel "Jimmy Jam" Harris III. But before that all happened, he would have a fortuitous meeting with a budding rock and roll musician from St. Paul's West Side and would get his first taste of local fame by joining a red-hot new band.

Chapter 3

RIVER ROAD BOOGIE

Well, you cross the bridge to Mendota, see
Way down deep to dig the scene
You're knocking on the door and you feel your best
A real crazy cat says, "Be my guest"
—"Be My Guest," Augie Garcia Quintet

One of the songs that played a recurring role in my early conversations with Cornbread was an original composition called "Chromosomes." A studio recording of the song appeared on his 2002 album *Cornbread Supreme, Volume 1,* and in the recording it starts out as a classic bebop shuffle, bright and rollicking, with room in the arrangement for vibrant saxophone, piano, and guitar solos. But a few minutes into the song, something strange happens: the entire band drops down to half time and then slows to a crawl, as if they are all suddenly trudging their way through six inches of mud. When Cornbread played it for me alone on the piano, he especially enjoyed lingering on the slower part of the composition and would let it fall out of time completely, stretching the tempo like taffy.

"That got to be one of my big hit tunes out there, when I played," he said. "People are like, what's he doing? Oh man, it just swells. Music is just such a wonderful thing, all by its own self."

It occurred to me one day, as I sat and listened to Cornbread deconstruct "Chromosomes," that the way he played the song bore an uncanny resemblance to the way he spoke about his past. While some stories were still just as vivid as the day they happened, he could no longer recall what year or even decade they may have occurred; an anecdote about an award he won or a venue he loved might be from five years ago or fifty. Did it matter? For a biographer maybe, but for everyone else, why should it?

Since he had reached his mid-nineties, Cornbread saw no reason to keep tempo when recalling his life; it all stretched out behind him like a rubber band that might snap back to the present moment at any instant. His memories came and went, depending on the week, and it didn't seem to bother him when he couldn't call up a particular name or venue or year. What mattered most to him was what was happening right in front of him.

"The only true thing is now," Cornbread liked to tell me. "And what's so killing is that it's always now!"

Anytime Cornbread got going on his thoughts about God and the universe, which would happen at least once every time we got together, he liked to preach about the concept of eternity. "People have a hard time considering eternity," he said, ramping up into a mini-sermon. "No end, no beginning, it's all the time. So, here we are: what time do you want to be there, what time you gotta go to bed, what time you gotta get up? All this kind of stuff. You kind of forget about eternity, that this has always been going on."

The past didn't seem so long ago to Cornbread, even though he'd experienced so much of it. Whether he was talking about the war, or his childhood trauma, or an especially joyful gig he just played last week, Cornbread spoke of it all like it just happened—because in a way, when measured in the grand scheme of everything that ever happened and ever will on this planet and everywhere else, it just did.

Which might help to explain why anytime we spoke about Cornbread's time playing with Augie Garcia's band—and especially when we listened to the precious few recordings that existed of the group—Cornbread seemed to come completely untethered to the present day and fall back through the decades, speaking as if he were still standing behind his piano at the River Road Club back in 1954, working the low end of the piano while his friend Augie danced and hollered away in front of him. A moment later, he would snap back to his piano bench and our conversation and take a moment to marvel at the fact that any of that happened to him at all.

As we got to know each other better and I learned to navigate Cornbread's unique state of mind, it became clear that the music offered a key to a door that had long been locked. For Cornbread, the songs were inextricably tied to his memories, and the memories brought back every detail of the music. His time with Augie remained one of his most treasured life experiences, and watching him recall it was electric.

THE FIRST TIME Cornbread and I discussed the Augie Garcia Quintet, we were still meeting at his daycare facility and I was just learning how to hunt down the group's long out-of-print records. When I handed him an old photograph of Augie and the band playing at the River Road Club, the memories came rushing back.

"Augie and the drummer were the original founders," Cornbread recalled, taking me all the way back to the beginning. "I was working at American Hoist and Derrick, downtown St. Paul, on one of them streets just after you cross the bridge over the river," he continued, referring to an area of St. Paul known as the West Side. "And across from where I worked was a bar. And instead of going right home, I went over to the bar—and the drummer and him were in the bar. And if the bar's still there, I can remember the booth that we sat in to talk about him having a band."

The drummer that Cornbread met on that momentous day was Johnny Lopez, who, like Augie Garcia, had grown up on the West Side and had just gotten out of the Army after serving in the Korean War. Unbeknownst to Cornbread at the time, Augie had already earned a reputation in the city for his performance of traditional Mexican *boleros* and *corridos* on acoustic guitar. After

47

he returned from serving overseas, he became curious about the emerging, electric sound of rock and roll.

As Cornbread remembered it, their initial conversation as a trio was pretty straightforward: "Oh, I'm a drummer." "Oh, I'm a guitar player!" "Oh, I'm a piano player!" they each said, discovering they had the ingredients for a basic rock band. Garcia had already secured a gig playing at the River Road Club down in Mendota, Minnesota, just a few miles down the Mississippi River from the bar where they all met, and before they finished their drinks Cornbread had an invitation to dust off the club's old piano and join them onstage.

Before he got to the gig, even the experience of driving to the club was its own adventure, Cornbread remembered. "The River Road Club—it was between the two cities. You had to go to the end of West Seventh and turn in at the top of the hill, and there was a club there where Dixieland music was being played," he said, possibly recalling Red Dougherty's Dixieland club Parker House or Doc Evans's South Rampart Street Club. "And when you drove through there, it was like driving through the parking lot of that club, and then you go down the hill to a dirt road. And I couldn't figure out how people could go on that road. I remember it as a one-track thing. And you drove and drove down this dirt road, you got to the end, like a peninsula-type thing, and this club was sitting at the back edge of the peninsula."

Today not only does the building that housed the River Road Club no longer exist, but the very land it sat on has been washed away. According to Dakota County historian Dave Byrne, the Corps of Engineers actually rerouted the area where the Mississippi River converges with the Minnesota River in the mid-1960s following a flood that wiped out the River Road Club, creating a channel that separates the site of the club from the bank of the river where it once was precariously perched. The land is now home to a hiking trail and recreational area called Picnic Island and is part of Fort Snelling State Park.

Archival photographs from the late 1950s show a small, incon-

Augie Garcia and saxophonist Willy Brown jump on Cornbread's piano while he plays the keys at the River Road Club, where the Augie Garcia Quintet performed several nights a week in 1954 and 1955. Augie Garcia Photograph Collection. Courtesy of the Minnesota Historical Society.

spicuous building, like a roadside tavern that one might happen upon while driving through a small town. But inside, for nearly every night of the week in 1954, 1955, and 1956, it was home to some of the sweatiest, most energetic underground rock and roll shows that the Twin Cities had ever seen.

Once the founding members of the Augie Garcia Quintet got together (including Cornbread, Augie, Johnny Lopez, the bassist Teddy Guzman, and Cornbread's friend Willy Brown on saxophone), they got to work creating their own spin on the rock and roll sound, with Cornbread heavily influencing the rhythm of the group.

"Jimmie Harris was the first piano player we had at the River Road Club in 1954," Augie Garcia recalled in 1996, speaking to a videographer before playing a reunion show with most of his old band. "And it was his rhythm and blues style, with that kind of a shuffle, that really took off for a lot of us. And singing a lot of the tunes that he basically taught me, [like] 'Going to Chicago.'"

"Going to Chicago," originally written by Count Basie and his orchestra vocalist Jimmy Rushing in 1941 and released as "Going to Chicago Blues," had been a treasured song in Cornbread's repertoire and a defining influence on his early sound, and he had been eager to share it with his new bandmates in the Augie Garcia Quintet. Not only is "Going to Chicago" one of the handful of songs that the group recorded in the 1950s, but it also laid the foundation for the quintet's biggest hit, "Hi Ho Silver," which was released with the typo "Hi Yo Silver" in 1955 as a 45 along with "Going to Chicago" on the B-side. Although the band didn't realize it at the time, their 45 was historic: it has since been regarded as the first rock and roll record to come out of the state of Minnesota.

Cornbread first told me about his love for "Going to Chicago" and the way it shaped their song "Hi Ho Silver" when he visited me at MPR back in 2018.

"I think about that often," he said. "I'm going along with Augie on the set, and I'm on this"—he stopped, cutting himself off midsentence to launch into "Going to Chicago" on the piano. "So I was doing this with the band," he explained, singing, "'Going to Chicago, sorry that I can't take you. Going to Chicago, sorry that I can't take you. 'Cause there ain't nothing in Chicago that a monkey woman like you can do.' So several choruses in, Augie takes over the thing, 'cause he's the leader of the group. And I'm in the background doing my thing. And he comes in talking 'bout 'Six more months, we're going on the road, baby.' To my song!

He starts murdering my song. 'Six more months, we're going on the road, baby. Don't ask me where I'm going, 'cause I don't know, baby.'"

As Cornbread told it, Augie kept vamping on the beat of the song and singing more improvised lyrics about how they would be hitting the road for Chicago, and they eventually landed on a new chorus: "We're singing Hi Ho, Hi Ho Silver, Hi Ho, Hi Ho Silver away."

"So 'Hi Ho Silver'—he ruined my song," Cornbread concluded, mocking disdain and laughing.

A few years later, as Cornbread and I focused our time together on digging into this period of his life, I became determined to find the band's original recording of "Going to Chicago" so he and I could listen to it again. I then found out just how rare this recording is despite its historic status. At the time it wasn't available on any streaming services or YouTube, so I spent weeks scouring eBay and Discogs until I finally managed to order a scratched-up copy of the original 7-inch record.

Even playing a record for Cornbread proved to be a challenge. He no longer had a turntable in his home, and I didn't have an easy way to bring one to him, so I ended up playing the record on my own turntable at home and recording it to video on my phone, then setting up a Bluetooth speaker on Cornbread's dining room table so I could crank it up loud enough for him to hear it clearly.

Cornbread chuckled at the combination of old- and new-school technology that I'd managed to cobble together in order for us to hear the record, and as soon as I hit play and the familiar crackle of the needle hitting the wax filled the air, he closed his eyes and floated away.

"Man, that is a memory," he said once the song finished. "I came and made the band swing, and then I hired the saxophone guy. Willy Brown, that horn player? He died young. I mean, he was on the way to be one of the greats, and he was just beginning to blow when he was coming with Augie. I could hear the future with the way he was developing and blowing."

Released in 1955, the Augie Garcia hit "Hi Ho Silver" also contains the B-side "Going to Chicago," a cover that was sung (uncredited) by Cornbread Harris. Courtesy of the author.

After we listened to the song a second time, something occurred to me: even though the record was scratchy and skipped, I started to clearly make out two separate voices on the track—a slightly lower, more soulful voice that sang the opening lines, and a higher voice that closed out the track.

"Cornbread, is that you singing in the beginning?" I asked.

"Well, yeah!" Cornbread said, as if we'd already discussed it multiple times. "That's what I'm saying, 'Going to Chicago'—that's where 'Hi Ho Silver' came from."

"Well, I didn't know you sang the lead melody," I added.

"Oh, well, hey. I tell ya, I'm so far ahead of myself I don't know half of the time," he said, giggling and clapping his hands. "You've been bringing stuff to me where I say, 'No, I didn't do that.' And you say, 'Well, yes you did!'"

Learning that Cornbread sang the majority of the melody on "Going to Chicago" was a revelation. Not only was he the co-songwriter on the state's first rock and roll recording, but he was also the uncredited performer of the B-side. Which meant that his entire recorded discography, beginning with those watershed recordings from 1955 with Augie Garcia and extending all the way up to the work he'd just done in the studio with the Peterson brothers in 2021, spanned a whopping sixty-six years.

During a separate visit, I'd managed to cobble together the rest of the Augie Garcia Quintet's recordings, which included six tracks recorded for the local North Star label—"Hi Ho Silver," "Going to Chicago," "Hello Baby," "Drinking Wine, Spoli Oli," "Ring-A-Ling-A," and a song that directly references their River Road Club shows, "Be My Guest"—plus two tracks released by the Kirk label, "Ivy League Baby" and "Let the Good Times Roll," that were recorded after Cornbread left the band. The first batch of songs were recorded in a house on Payne Avenue in St. Paul, with most of the band sharing a single microphone. Listening to the old recordings together, especially "Be My Guest," brought Cornbread right back to those nascent days.

"That's it!" Cornbread exclaimed, singing along and clapping his hands to the beat as Augie sang, "Well, you cross the bridge to Mendota, see / Way down deep to dig the scene / You're knocking on the door and you feel your best / A real crazy cat says, 'Be my guest.'" In addition to the nostalgic lyrics about the River Road Club, the "Be My Guest" recording is defined by Cornbread's relentless, driving boogie-woogie piano beat and includes a notable piano solo by him halfway through the song.

"Man, I was tickling those ivories! Oh man," he said. "That's all a spur-of-the-moment arrangement. No books, no pages, nothing. Just wing it, and then still come together like that. And that sounds very close-up and personal. It doesn't sound like the older recordings that have this kind of ethereal, faraway feel. This seems like *right there*."

As Cornbread remembered it, most of the songs were recorded in a single day, and in a single take. "I don't think we went into the studio but once, actually, and the studio was a house, upstairs and downstairs. We recorded our music at that house. One take. That kind of thing ingrained in me when I started recording: sometimes we would rehearse and sometimes we wouldn't, but when we got to the studio, that was it."

THE EARLY BUZZ that the band garnered playing the River Road Club was only amplified once they released their first records, especially as "Hi Ho Silver" garnered some local airplay. He could still remember the experience of hearing his band on the car radio for the first time. Cornbread said it seemed like they were playing nearly every night, and throngs of teenagers and young adults would pack the dance floor.

The band knew how to make a strong impression, too. Augie was a natural showman with a unique presence onstage, which Cornbread said was influenced by his day job working for Ramsey County. "He was a lineman," Cornbread recalled, "climbing telephone poles and stuff, and fixing electric for the people." So once Augie got onstage, he had no problem hopping up on top of Cornbread's piano while he played. "He could dance on the piano in his Bermuda shorts, that was part of the show. And people came to see that happen," Cornbread remembered. "He walked the rail between the bar and the dance floor, and then there was a walkway in between—he'd walk the rail like a tightrope walker and still be playing."

In a *Minneapolis Morning Tribune* review of an Augie Garcia show in March 1955 titled "Under the Bridge Hides a Hot Guitar," entertainment columnist Will Jones expanded on Augie's incomparable live act. "Garcia works in Bermuda shorts, pink-and-charcoal argyle socks, a sleeveless kind of pink toga, and a pair of moccasins that look like sacks. He plays a guitar that could have been designed by Salvador Dali," Jones wrote. "His quartet includes a drummer with a loud, relentless beat and a piano player who stands up while playing."

After I read this clipping to Cornbread, I asked him if he remembered standing up behind his piano. "Yeah, I did that," he said matter-of-factly. "But I finally managed to sit down."

The review continued: "A college-age crowd keeps the dance floor jammed. They work, too, and enjoy it. They were pretty tolerant about letting a couple of pairs of old married folks two-step around the edge of the dance floor, the better to observe the fun. . . . Garcia plays Friday, Saturday, Sunday and Wednesday nights."

"How about that?" Cornbread said. "Four nights a week. I mean, we packed that place! And the only problem was he didn't have a fence around the parking lot. And then someone drove off into the river, and that was the end of it. The girls died. That was really bad."

Not long after Augie's rave review in the *Minneapolis Morning Tribune,* in the fall of 1955, a tragedy struck the River Road Club when a group of six young women piled into their car after a show one night and skidded down the riverbank and into the water. Despite desperate attempts to rescue the women from the submerged vehicle, five of the passengers ended up drowning that night, and only one survived.

Cornbread said the accident effectively ended their popular residency at the club, but the band continued at other venues, including bars on West Seventh Street in St. Paul and the Prom Ballroom, which was becoming a popular site for teen dances in that era.

Before he left the group, Cornbread would take part in the most high-profile gig of Augie Garcia's career: opening for none other than the King of Rock and Roll. "I grounded Elvis Presley," Cornbread told me, speaking somewhat sheepishly about it while

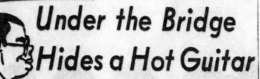

AFTER LAST NIGHT   **By Will Jones**

Under the Bridge Hides a Hot Guitar

Just finding the River Road club, a beer joint that lies at the end of a narrow road that winds along the river under the Mendota bridge, is a small accomplishment in itself.

Once you get there—as I did over the week-end—the reward comes in the form of a short, barrel-chested guitar player named Augie Garcia.

GARCIA WORKS in Bermuda shorts, pink-and-charcoal argyle socks, a sleeveless kind of pink toga, and a pair of moccasins that look like sacks. He plays a guitar that could have been designed by Salvador Dali.

His quartet includes a drummer with a loud, relentless beat and a piano player who stands up while playing. They work under a dim blue spotlight.

Garcia hunches over his guitar in an ape-like pose, sweats profusely, and hoarsely chants such inspired lyrics as "Drinkin' wine, spo-dee o-dee."

A college-age crowd keeps the dance floor jammed. They work, too, and enjoy it. They were pretty tolerant about letting a couple of pairs of old married folks two-step around the edge of the dance floor, the better to observe the fun.

In fact, I get bumped and shoved less on that dance floor than I do in the Flame room. Garcia plays Friday, Saturday, Sunday and Wednesday nights.

Debbie   K. T. Stevens
Reynolds
Two tender traps

gave up after wasting two or three nickels.

We went through most of the rolls stacked on the top of the piano—older items like "Barney Google," "If You Knew Susie," and "Rose Marie," newer ones like "The Old Piano Roll Blues" and the air corps song, and any number of Polish numbers.

Trying to read Polish on a piano roll as it whizzes by, reading from bottom to top, is, easily as good a Sunday afternoon diversion as Prizeword Pete.

"If you can think of a better way to spend Sunday afternoon," said my friend, "you name her."

I have to go along with his enthusiasm for the player piano. No beer joint should be without one. Or, for that matter, no home.

Augie Garcia and his live band earned a rave review in the *Minneapolis Morning Tribune* on March 29, 1955. The write-up by Will Jones offers an important documentation of the band's historic residency at the River Road Club. *Minneapolis Morning Tribune*, March 29, 1955. Courtesy of the Minnesota Historical Society.

This rare exterior photograph of the historic River Road Club in Mendota was taken for insurance purposes following the tragic accident that claimed the lives of five young women who were attending an Augie Garcia show there in 1955. Courtesy of the Dakota County Historical Society.

bringing it up unprompted one day. "He tried to fly high through the Twin Cities, and they ended up getting Augie Garcia for an opener. We blew him away."

ELVIS PRESLEY MADE HIS TWIN CITIES DEBUT on Sunday, May 13, 1956, playing both the St. Paul and Minneapolis auditoriums in a single day. For his afternoon matinee in St. Paul, the Augie Garcia Quintet was chosen as one of the opening acts— and as legend has it, the hot local band with a regional radio hit whipped up the audience of young music fans so successfully that Elvis's notoriously controlling manager Colonel Tom Parker personally insisted that they cut the set short so they didn't upstage the young star.

Young women scream in anticipation of seeing Elvis Presley at the St. Paul Auditorium on May 13, 1956. As the opening act, the Augie Garcia Quintet had young women "standing on their chairs" and were yanked offstage for causing too much fervor. Minneapolis and St. Paul Newspaper Negatives Collection, n.p., 1956. Courtesy of the Minnesota Historical Society.

Both Cornbread and Augie wore this incident like a badge of honor. Speaking to the *Star Tribune* about it in 1993, Augie recalled that Parker "pulled me off stage by my jacket. There wasn't supposed to be any competition." The frenzy of the crowd was even documented by the *St. Paul Pioneer Press*, a reporter for which was there to cover Elvis's show. "They started screaming when Augie Garcia, local rock and roll idol, started playing at 2:30 p.m.," the newspaper reported. "By 2:50 p.m. they were standing on the chairs."

In a separate interview Augie conducted with *Insider* magazine in the early 1970s, he expanded on his memories of the concert. "When Elvis Presley made his first Minneapolis appearance, he kind of laid an egg," Augie said. "They were expecting thousands and thousands of people, but mostly what filled it up was my friends. I could see them down in front from the stage."

"Oh, we're never going to live that down!" Cornbread said. "Augie, man. And of course it was our fans, and so we automatically played good for them. And then they appreciated us more than they did Elvis. Oh. That's historical."

With the band at the height of their popularity, there was a tension building within the group, Cornbread remembered. "Hi Ho Silver" had started gaining airplay not just in the Twin Cities but around the Midwest, and the band was eager to go on tour, much like the lyrics to the song foreshadowed ("In six more months, we're going on the road, baby"). In a 1981 interview with KTCA-TV's *Night Times Magazine* program, which is now archived at the Minnesota History Center, Augie said that they even had an offer on the table to go down to Chicago and perform at the Playboy Club, but that some of the members of the band had families and didn't want to travel.

In Cornbread's memory, the band started to lose momentum when the members turned over and their sound shifted. He said that when he left the group he was replaced by a piano player named Buddy Davis, who took things in a more jazz-oriented direction. By the '60s, audiences' tastes had changed again, and Augie eventually dissolved the group and returned to his day job.

Augie was diagnosed with throat cancer in 1993 and passed away in 1999 when he was only sixty-seven years old. Augie and Cornbread had the opportunity to reunite onstage one more time in April 1996, when they came together for a concert at the Prom Center with drummer Johnny Lopez, bassist Maurice Turner (who also happened to be Prince's uncle), and other former members of the Augie Garcia Quintet. A videotape of the reunion performance is now archived at the Minnesota History Center, and I had a chance to visit the Gale Library there to view it for myself. In the video, Augie is clearly pleased to see Cornbread again, lavishing praise on him before the show and asking

Happy Birthday Jimmy!

Sorry I can't be there tonight with you and your friends. I'm just not up to it yet. I'm getting better every day. Be the Good Lord willing we'll get together soon. Don't forget to play a few hot licks for me!

Love you pal,
Let the good times roll!

Your Amigo,
Augie!

An undated note from Augie Garcia to Cornbread from the mid- to late 1990s, around the time the two Minnesota music legends reconnected to play a reunion concert. Courtesy of Cornbread Harris.

him to talk about his new CD, *Live at Nikki's,* which was about to be released. Cornbread stands next to Augie and smiles shyly toward the camera, then looks around at the band and says, "You guys gotta play those Willy Brown riffs tonight."

The reunited band played two full sets of music, including all their old hits, and Cornbread had a chance to sing lead when it came time to do "Going to Chicago." Even on the grainy VHS tape, you can see the joy that the performance brought to the musicians and to the hundreds of baby boomers dancing away in the audience, like they were all taking a hard-earned victory lap. When I asked Cornbread about it, he said he no longer remembered playing the reunion concert or all the nice things Augie had said about him. "I was there? Good, I like that, I'm glad I was there," Cornbread said, smiling as he listened to me describe the tape. "Like I said when you started on this book and you started investigating—that's me? Man, I *knew* I was a blessed dude! I knew it."

IN MANY WAYS, the friction that built inside the Augie Garcia Quintet about whether or not to tour, and how to balance a musical life with a family life, foreshadowed one of Cornbread's core struggles in his music career. Though many of the details about his personal life in this period have long since faded away, we were able to figure out that Cornbread's first marriage to Dollie Schuck ended sometime during the Augie Garcia band's heyday or shortly after it, and that he married a new love interest, Bertha Lee Tate, in 1957, shortly before welcoming his second child in 1959. Cornbread and Bertha remained married until the mid-1970s and separated when their son, James Samuel "Jimmy Jam" Harris III, was a teenager.

"I do remember that my relationships had the tension in them," Cornbread said when I asked him about this period. "That's something for the psychiatrist to figure out," he added, cracking a wry smile.

It was fall by the time Cornbread and I finished piecing together his history in the 1950s, and we had been meeting at his home for several weeks. Away from the distractions of the daycare facility, we were really getting to know one another on a personal level, and he was starting to open up more about his life's hardships. By this point a few months had passed since he had his big reunion with Jimmy, and I could tell that the distance between them was still weighing heavily on his mind. As grateful as he was for that fleeting moment of love and forgiveness, he was hungry for more.

On Father's Day that year, Jimmy had extended a public olive branch to his dad: he had made an unusually personal Instagram post about how Cornbread had influenced him, sharing an old photograph of the two of them together and writing, "My musical talent came from my dad, who sacrificed his musical career to raise me so I could have mine." Without any additional communication from Jimmy, Cornbread had been left to play this message over and over again in his mind.

"That was because of Bertha getting on my case," Cornbread recalled, "saying, 'Come on now, you've got to be more of a dad to the kid.' And we weren't, you know, my son and I weren't that close, and then the breakup was because of me, and he has held that against me during this whole time. And then finally when he came to meet me now, he said he's sorry he held that against me, because that's part of why he didn't want to be bothered with me, because I mistreated his mother. And now, like I say, now I got the number and I can't get ahold of him."

Try as he might to reach Jimmy, the number he was given still wouldn't connect, and Cornbread was growing more frustrated the longer their silence endured. While I'd been hesitant to insert myself any further into the middle of their tenuous relationship, I eventually recognized that Cornbread, as he griped about the busy signals and strange messages each week, was trying to ask me to help.

"How would you feel if I reached out to him?" I asked.

"Oh, that would be fine," Cornbread replied, looking relieved. "Because that's how come we got to meet before: [it] was [because of] friends and relatives and fans. And he was actually leaving town that day, and he came over to the center and said, 'Hey, I was in town.' Well, I knew that because he's a big timer, so it was in the papers, see. But anyway, so we talked and hugged, but I never got any deeper than crying, you know."

"Well, I didn't want to reach out to him again without asking you first, because I want us to be on the same page," I said. "But I think he would be interested to know that we're working on a project about your life and that if he wants to be involved, the door is open."

"Yes, absolutely," Cornbread said, sighing and relaxing back into his chair. "Thank you so very, very, very much. And say,

62

'How come your dad's number doesn't come through? Because he's been really trying to call you.'"

As soon as I left Cornbread's house that day, I sent a text through the ether to Jimmy Jam and explained that I'd started working on a book about his dad. He wrote back right away: "Hey Andrea, hope you're good. I'm glad you're writing it and would love to be a part of it."

My heart leapt. I couldn't wait to tell Cornbread and to watch what might happen next. While there was no way to predict it at the time, that small text exchange was the start of a new chapter that would stretch on for weeks, and then months, and then years, weaving our three lives together in beautiful, unexpected ways.

Chapter 4

DEEPER BLUES

Put him through some changes
Make him pay his dues
When you find out he really loves you
Teach him the deeper blues
—"Deeper Blues," Cornbread Harris

By the time the first leaves began to fall off the trees and crunch underfoot that autumn, Cornbread and I had settled into a predictable routine that we both seemed to look forward to and enjoy. Every Tuesday afternoon around 1:30 p.m., I would ring him up to tell him that I was heading over. No matter the time of day, he always answered the phone the same way: "Good morning, good morning!"

"How are you doing today, Cornbread?" I'd ask.

Without missing a beat, he would reply, "Exquisite."

A short while later, I'd pull up in front of his house and make my way up the front steps and onto the porch, where I'd wait for anywhere from a minute to ten minutes for him to hear me and make his way to the door. In an effort to announce my presence, I'd started rapping my knuckles on the door frame to the beat of "Shave and a Haircut," TAP-ta-ta-TAP-TAP, until I heard the floorboards creaking on the other side of the door. Without fail, he always tapped back before opening the door—TAP-TAP—and I could hear him giggling to himself as he fumbled with the lock and swung it open. Before opening the outer door he would lean up against the screen and ask, "Is that you?" And I would always reply, "It's me!"

Cornbread loved this little bit of call-and-response. By the time I sat down to write this book, we'd probably done it dozens of times. It was a playful, musical way to say hello, and in many ways it mirrored the way Cornbread approached his life's work.

The more I studied Cornbread's back catalog and learned about the Black cultural traditions he helped to develop and sustain, the more it became obvious to me that call-and-response had been a foundational element of his music for several decades. Beginning with songs like Augie Garcia Quintet's "Drinking Wine, Spoli Oli," in which the band shouted out "Wine, wine, wine" and Cornbread responded with "Chokecherry, raspberry, blackberry," and leading up to the way he traded lines with his band on the choruses of "Cherry Red" or "When the Saints Go Marching In" in his most recent live performances, Cornbread thrived when he was beckoning everyone around him to join in and participate in his joyful sound.

Call-and-response has a rich history that dates back centuries and is a fundamental part of the Black musical canon. From ancient African tribal songs to work songs of enslaved African Americans, and from Black preachers calling out to their deacons and congregations to A Tribe Called Quest's Q-Tip asking "Can I kick it?" and a chorus of voices responding, "Yes you can," call-and-response is a defining characteristic of Black music and a powerful way that artists and cultural workers across generations have cultivated a sense of unity.

"Black Music is a collective experience, not a fixed object—and should be appreciated as such," the musician Adam Longman Parker, best known as Afriqua, noted when writing about call-and-response for Ableton.com. "The 'Yes Lawd!' interjected during a gospel performance, the hollers of excitement that accompany a big drop during a techno party, or the boos at a weak number on *Showtime at the Apollo* are not merely incidental, but in fact integral parts of the Black Music experience. The performers express themselves with their interpretation of the music, and respond to one another's musical whims. The audience responds in real time, thereby becoming a part of the music making process."

Eventually I, too, became a part of Cornbread's music-making process, as he cajoled me into singing along with him as he played his piano. I also became a part of another song he was composing as we worked together: the one where Jimmy was back in his life in a more consistent way, and the one where he could eventually look over and see his son next to him again onstage.

Though Cornbread longed to be connected more immediately to Jimmy and find a way for the two of them to sing in harmony, in many ways his early period of reconciliation with his son resembled an extended bit of call-and-response. That fall, under Cornbread's supervision, I began speaking to one of them and then another, bringing their messages back and forth like a carrier pigeon, observing how each of them began to gain more of an understanding of the other until the point they were ready to be connected in real time.

After Jimmy texted me back to say that he was interested in being involved in Cornbread's story, I suggested that we find a time to connect over video chat so I could fill him in on how things were going and learn more about what memories he'd like to share. As it turned out, he had quite a lot to say. That first call stretched on for more than two hours, and I learned that he had been holding on to surprisingly detailed memories of his childhood and all the things he learned from Cornbread personally, socially, and musically.

SO MANY OF JIMMY'S MEMORIES were about small moments shared with his dad—the kind of stuff that doesn't seem remarkable in the moment but becomes more special as the years slip by. He remembered watching Cornbread perfectly reheat his leftovers the morning after a gig and sneaking a taste of the results;

67

watching him work on his cars; going with his dad to the race-track in Brainerd and driving their own car down the drag strip on an open day; and going together to the local airports to watch the planes take flight.

As he spoke about these early memories, I couldn't help but bring up a song Cornbread wrote about his son, "Cool Rider," which had long been a staple of his live sets and appears on more than one of his CDs. It's a bittersweet ode to long-lost days and a tale of a son who had flown so high he was out of reach. Every time Cornbread played it, he dedicated it to Jimmy.

Started on the drag strip
Motorcycle hill
He set a brand-new record
When he drove at Bonneville
Ride on (ride on)

Ride on (ride on)
Ride on (ride on)
Ride on, cool rider, you know you're real, real gone

He went up in a jet plane
A hundred miles out
And when that kid got back
You should have heard the people shout

Ride on (ride on)
Ride on (ride on)
Ride on (ride on)
Ride on, cool rider, you know you're real, real gone

Went up in a rocket ship
Lots of smoke and dust
And written on the rocket ship
"To the moon or bust"

Ride on (ride on)
Ride on (ride on)

Ride on (ride on)
Ride on, cool rider, you know you're real, real gone

"That song sounds familiar to me," Jimmy said. "That was one of the things we loved: we loved drag racing, we loved racing of all kinds. We would go to the little local races, watch the Indy 500 and all of those kinds of things." When I held a CD up to the computer screen for Jimmy to see, he nodded his head and recalled getting a copy somewhere along the way, possibly back in 2001 when *Cornbread Supreme, Volume 1* was first released. "I vaguely remember it, but it also would have been at a point where I would have been aware of it, but I wouldn't have been necessarily accepting to listen to it, or excited to listen to it," he commented frankly.

Some of Jimmy's memories of his dad were more sparse. He didn't remember learning anything about Cornbread's parents or the fact that they had died when his dad was so young, or ever knowing much about their extended family beyond his mother Bertha's children from a previous marriage. He didn't know where his dad went to school or grew up. "I don't know if there was so much that I didn't ask, or if he just didn't share those types of things," he said. But what he did know is that somehow, without needing to know any of those things, he and his dad had grown into two adults who were remarkably alike.

"One of the things I know that I take from him is that whenever we're at an event, like the Grammys or wherever, we're always the last ones to leave," Jimmy reflected, chuckling. "And I remember being young, and I remember saying to him, 'Do you have to talk to everybody that's here?' And he was always like, 'You never know where people have come from, and that might be their only time seeing me.' So now my kids are subjected to the same thing."

Jimmy also pinpointed a shared tendency toward getting lost in a moment and forgetting to tend to the more practical, mundane aspects of life. He remembered a day when his dad was driving him to Field Elementary School one morning in his powder blue Karmann Ghia, which they both loved. "About a block from the house it breaks down," Jimmy recalled. "The school is maybe five blocks away, six blocks away. And instead of going to school, I'm sitting there watching him tinker with the car. Tinker, tinker, tinker, tinker, tinker. We walk back home, and I remember my mom going, 'Why aren't you at school?' And I said, 'The car broke down.' And she said, 'Well, why didn't you just walk to school?' I was what, seven, eight years old. I was totally capable of walking to school. I just didn't think about it," he continued, noting that Cornbread didn't think of it either. "I just wanted to watch him tinker and figure out how to fix the car."

Jimmy chuckled while recalling how he still seemed to end up in these situations as an adult. "That kind of, I don't know, lack of thinking, or I don't even know what I would call it. I still have that sometimes with my kids," he continued. "I blame it on my creative spirit. And that was the way my dad was."

The more he spoke, the bigger Cornbread's influence seemed to loom over Jimmy's own life. "A lot of decisions I made in my life were because of things that I felt were taken from him, like the ability to do music for such a long time, because he was raising me and had to work a regular job and wasn't able to take gigs that he wanted to take," he shared matter-of-factly. "It was important for me to say to him that I don't blame him. I mean, life happens the way it happens, but I have no blame or resentment or anything."

With the past behind them, it created the possibility for something new: a chance for Jimmy to learn about where he came from, and how he got from a regular childhood on the South Side of Minneapolis to a star-studded life in Beverly Hills, filled with A-list recording sessions, countless Grammy awards, and—during the course of collaborating with Cornbread and me on this book—an induction into the Rock and Roll Hall of Fame. "That's the thing that makes me curious: I don't know how he got to that point and the lessons that he taught me. I don't know

DEEPER BLUES

how he learned those lessons," Jimmy said. "But I just know that every day in my life that I make music, it's because of him."

The more time I spent with Jimmy, the more I understood that he and his father did indeed share a lot of the same personality traits and quirks. They were both extroverts and natural-born performers who thrived in social settings and yet spoke to the person in front of them with a laser focus, never rushing their way through an interaction. In fact, when left to their own devices they could each talk for hours about music, about life, and about all the lessons they'd learned along the way, to whomever was within earshot to listen. They were both spiritual and felt a strong connection between their faith in music and faith in God. And they both loved to quote scripture; for Cornbread, most of his favorite guiding principles came from the Bible. For Jimmy, they'd come from his lifelong business partner and best friend, Terry Lewis. "It's like Terry always says to me, 'It's not your fault, but it's your problem,'" Jimmy liked to say, quoting one of Terry's many mantras while reflecting on the ups and downs of his childhood.

Jimmy and I spent a lot of our first interview together unpacking the many complex feelings that he had about his parents' separation—which wasn't his fault but definitely was his problem, and one that chased him through most of his adult life. Jimmy said he was a teenager when his parents split, but the seeds of discontent were planted years before. From Jimmy's vantage point, the big turning point in Cornbread's marriage to Bertha and his own development as a budding musician happened simultaneously one weekend in 1970, when Cornbread was invited to visit a recording studio and sit in as a session player for the artist James Bonner.

"This was, you know, one of the pivotal kind of moments," Jimmy said. "He was working with this guy James Bonner. And he had a song called 'Don't Rush It.' And James was the actual artist, but my dad was going to play keyboard with him on the song. What I remember was he had this recording session. I remember it was a Saturday and a Sunday. And of course I went,

In 1970, Cornbread was invited to contribute to a recording session for the artist James Bonner and brought his eleven-year-old son Jimmy along. This was Jimmy's first time in a recording studio. Courtesy of Cornbread Harris.

because of course I'm going, right? And I remember being in the drum booth. I was young, but I could play the drums a little bit. And I remember going in and playing the drums. I'm sure I was driving these people crazy. I was that kid that was driving people crazy. Because I was beating on whatever, and I'd get on the piano and play."

Jimmy would have been eleven years old at the time of the session. It goes without saying, considering how many sessions he's been a part of since that fateful day, that Jimmy's first visit to a recording studio made a strong impression. All these years later, he could still recall the lyrics of the song and hum the melody of "Don't Rush It," with its main chorus instructing the listener, "Don't rush it / Take a little time and be sure that you're sure of it."

"I remember them going through like a bunch of different takes, and learning the song and playing it. I thought it was a cool

Another angle in the recording studio captures Jimmy Harris *(far left)* watching Cornbread *(behind the organ)* as the musicians set up for a recording session with James Bonner. Courtesy of Cornbread Harris.

song," Jimmy continued. "And then I remember later on when the record came out, I remember my dad got, you know, some 45s to the house. And it was a big argument that happened because the record was kind of taking off a little bit—it was sort of a regional hit, you'd hear it on the radio. And he worked at a place called Grease and Hydraulics, and he had enough tenure where he could take three months or six months off. He could take a leave of absence and still walk back into the job. And I remember him and my mom arguing about it. And I always was aware how much my dad loved music. That was like his thing, you know? And I remember my mom going, you know, 'Well, you said you weren't gonna do music anymore, and now you want to leave your job, and you have a son, and blah, blah, blah.' It was this whole thing. And this was nights and nights and nights."

The tension continued to build, Jimmy recalled, spurred on by alcohol and resentment. "I mean, the whole idea of alcoholism and those types of things, it was a different thing. But my mom had a pattern. And every night, it turned into, in my mind, basically just a bash fest of what he wasn't doing. The major thing was the music thing, because she was like, 'You said you were going to give up music and work a regular job,' and whatever, which I'm sure he did say, and I'm sure he had intentions of doing. But even as a nine-year-old or ten-year-old, or whatever I was at that point, I knew that couldn't happen. Like, music should be happening in his life. Because that was the way I felt about music."

CORNBREAD MARRIED BERTHA LEE TATE on December 30, 1957. Both Cornbread and Bertha had been married previously and had children from their other marriages, but Jimmy remembers growing up alone in their home with them on Portland Avenue in South Minneapolis and essentially being raised as an only child.

Bertha was born in Fergus Falls, Minnesota, and was connected to the historic lineage of Black families known as the First 85 who migrated to Fergus Falls from Kentucky in 1897 and created the area's first African American community. Born in 1918, Bertha was almost ten years older than Cornbread. She had previously married Ray Webster in Otter Tail County in 1935 and had three children, Eugene, Donna, and Milton, before moving to Minneapolis, where she became a private school teacher and later a Head Start teacher and tutor for Minneapolis Public Schools. She was an active member of the South Minneapolis community, contributing to the *Minneapolis Spokesman-Recorder*, teaching Sunday school at Grace Trinity Presbyterian Church, and volunteering at Sabathani Community Center.

She was also an early booster of Jimmy's burgeoning music career. He remembers his mother acting as his de facto manager and guiding him as he booked his first gigs, including his time gigging as a drummer in Cornbread's trio, Huckleberry Finn, Cornbread and a Friend, when Jimmy was only twelve years old.

Eventually, after years of growing friction between his parents, Cornbread moved out of the house. Jimmy estimated he was about fifteen at the time. "It wasn't a knock-down-drag-out thing, you know. I never hated him," Jimmy recalled. "It was never anything like that. It just was more circumstances. You know, he went a different way at a certain point. And it was just me and my mom, and it was like, 'Okay, well, we'll figure it out.' And we figured it out."

Over the years Cornbread and Jimmy's separation grew into an estrangement—one that wasn't so much the result of a single moment but, rather, a long, quiet, passive avoidance of one another that stretched on through the rest of Jimmy's adolescence, kept going through his early career success performing as a deejay and in Prince's protégé act The Time, and persevered throughout his ascent to superstardom as part of the hit-making producer duo Jam and Lewis.

Looking back on his childhood five decades later, Jimmy was certain that what happened between his parents—and, specifically, what happened as a result of that one-off recording session with James Bonner—forever altered the trajectory of his life. "That planted, for me, my sort of direction. My intention was, 'I'm never getting married, and I'm never having kids.' That's why. Those evenings of arguments and watching him not being able to do what he wanted to do, made me like, *I'm not gonna give that up.* I love music too much to do that. So that affected my life more so than him, you know, leaving when he left. Because the leaving—when he left, I was already on that path in my mind, that music is what I'm going to do. And I was going to try to make a living doing it before I tried to do anything else.

"It was funny because I remember Terry always used to say I had an off switch. And my off switch was always, you know, when I was with a girl, and at some point in time, they would say, 'You love your music more than you love me.' And that was always like, nope, you're done. Because for me, music wasn't something I liked or loved. Music was oxygen. So it was like saying, 'You love

An advertisement for Cornbread's residency with his trio Huckleberry Finn, Cornbread and Friends (sometimes printed as Huckleberry Finn, Cornbread and a Friend) ran in the *Minneapolis Star,* January 17, 1974.

oxygen more than you love me?' Well, yeah, I do as a matter of fact, because I need it to live, you know? I need oxygen to live, I need water to live, I need food to live—I need music to live. That's the way I felt about it. And that was the way my dad was. So to watch that opportunity be taken from him really affected all my decision making in my life."

Of course, Jimmy did eventually find a way to have both music and family in his life. He said that his wife, Lisa Padilla, whom he married in 1994, was the first woman he met who accepted the fact that music played such a dominant role in his daily existence and encouraged him not to let his childhood experiences prevent him from becoming a loving husband and father. He is now the dad to three adult children, including a son, Max, who is especially eager to follow in his predecessors' footsteps and pursue a life in music. Jimmy brought Max with him when he visited Cornbread at the daycare facility that day in May 2021 to show his dad that the musical tradition was alive and that everyone turned out okay.

As Jimmy remembered it, that James Bonner session was a turning point, but it wasn't the end of his relationship with his dad. Before Cornbread moved out of their family home, he and Jimmy would enjoy a few years of making music together, both at home and on stages around Minneapolis and Lake Minnetonka.

ARMED WITH JIMMY'S RECOLLECTIONS and the names of a few venues where they once shared a stage, I went back to Cornbread's house to see what he would make of it all. As soon as we took our places in Cornbread's dining room, I started telling him about everything I'd learned.

"I have some good news," I said. "Yesterday I had a really long, good conversation with Jimmy."

"Jimmy . . . Jam?!" Cornbread responded excitedly.

"Yes! He had so many wonderful things to say about you," I replied.

"What?! That's amazing, because he didn't speak to me for about twenty-four years," Cornbread said, shaking his head.

I started asking Cornbread about some of the venues Jimmy had mentioned, where he had remembered playing early gigs with his dad. "Do you remember a club out on Lake Minnetonka called the Surfside?" I asked.

"Oh wow. Oh! Yeah, yeah!" he said, looking at me with wonder. "But I didn't remember until just now. Like a flash of light, come pow! Wow. Okay, yeah, Lake Minnetonka. They had a guy playing out there, and I went out a couple times, 'Cornbread, sit in, sit in.' I mean he was *the* piano player, that dude could play. So I got up there and stumbled a little bit. So then he retired from there, and they called me up and asked could I come out and play. I'd guess I went out there to Mound, Minnesota, about eight or ten times."

"Interesting," I responded. "Well, it left a very strong impression on Jimmy."

"I doubted whether I left any impression on him or not, except, you know, me not getting along with his mother. That was the impression that kept him away for twenty-four years," Cornbread said, bowing his head.

As he thought about it more, he recognized that what he and Jimmy shared musically in those early days was quite special, even if it was fleeting. "Father, son, that was a big thing. People were catering to us a lot," he recalled. "Because of him, I got a lot of gigs, by having my son play with me, and I thought, boy, wouldn't it be a wonderful thing to come now? Us playing together someplace, somewhere, sometime."

With his thoughts racing between the early 1970s and the present, I asked Cornbread whether he remembered playing with a gentleman named James Bonner and helping him to record a song called "Don't Rush It." To help jog his memory, I pulled up a YouTube video I found of someone playing the 45 and turned the volume all the way up.

"That fits me to a T," Cornbread said, nodding his approval as the song played. The recording was dominated by a strumming electric guitar part and Bonner's soulful voice, but a layering of horns and Cornbread's organ part could be heard in the background supporting the melody. "That's my kind of thing. I was sure kicking it. I knew at the early stages, don't try to hog it—give back to the singer and give them a boost. Cooperate with the other people. Once that cooperation got going and we started having these musical conversations, that was it."

Cornbread and Jimmy's momentous visit to the studio together in 1970 resulted in the James Bonner 45 "Don't Rush It" b/w "Stumpin'," released in January 1971. Courtesy of the author.

I asked whether Cornbread remembered what happened after that session, including the 45s being sent to the home and the band being invited to go out on tour. When I brought up the friction that built in his marriage after that, he bowed his head again.

"Oh yeah, amen," Cornbread said. "People start talking about going on tour, and oh God, here we go. I already take a lot of extra time that normally people don't take, as far as my music, away from the family."

The more I filled Cornbread in on what Jimmy said, the clearer his memories about his conflict with Bertha became. It was also not lost on either of us how cyclical this kind of battle had been in his life, as he attempted to juggle his home life with his dedication to his craft over the decades. He spoke about the conflict fluidly, as if it might apply to his marriage to Bertha or his previous marriage to Dollie Shuck, which crumbled during the Augie Garcia days.

"Oh yeah. Music was not an acceptable way of making a living, as far as she was concerned," he said. "And I was making a living five nights a week. You know? Man, money was just rolling in. Place was packed. But, you know, very few people can take what an artist does—especially when they glom into their art very deeply. That shuts out a lot of contact that you would have. So it was, 'Which would you rather have, a big band playing every night at some nice place, or a home and a family? Well, that isn't no decision even to make. It's already made! Music, music, music."

To bring the point home, Cornbread said that his feelings about marital strife were best encapsulated in his song "Deeper Blues," a song that he played at every gig just after his theme song "Blue Blue Blue Blues" and that he considered one of the crown jewels in his songwriting catalog.

Cornbread paused and slowly swiveled around on his piano bench, dipping his left shoulder down and squeezing his eyes closed as he played me an especially heartfelt rendition. Originally intended for a full band with horn arrangement, the blues ballad was the most profound when he played it alone at the piano, where he could revel in the tension that built up in the first few verses and then was released in the song's soaring chorus.

The point of attack is behind the back
Treat him any way that you choose
Take a little time off, don't hurry back
'Cause you ain't got nothin' to lose

Eat at his table, your children and you
You know that he's able and he wants to do for you
So dog him, you know you've got it made

Why don't you go ahead and hurt him—
And then ask him, "How you doin', babe?"

Never, never show him the way that you really feel
Never, never tell him that your love is not real
Promise to love him until the end
And when you leave, ask him, "Can we still be friends?"

Change your mind, apologize
Tell him you did not realize
Put him through some changes
Make him pay his dues
When you find out he really loves you
Teach him the deeper blues

Something shifted in Cornbread during that visit, as he listened to me explain what Jimmy had said and reflected on his own feelings about this tumultuous period in his life. Even though he and Jimmy hadn't communicated directly about it, it was clear that he found profound relief in knowing that his actions were understood by his son. When Jimmy came to him and told him he forgave him, Cornbread knew that he must have meant it with his whole heart, because he still remembered all the hardship alongside the joy of their reconnection.

Like storm clouds clearing, once Cornbread was able to express his feelings about the more difficult aspects of his separation from Jimmy and his mother, it opened up a new space in his mind to consider something he hadn't thought about in decades: that maybe he'd passed along more to Jimmy than heartache. Maybe he actually made some kind of positive impact on his life and played a part in shaping his globally recognized music career.

The idea of being recognized as a part of Jimmy Jam's musical legacy was thrilling to Cornbread, and he wanted to know more about what his son remembered. What songs did he teach Jimmy? What did it mean that he gave him his first gigs? And was there actually a possibility that they could play together again?

On Father's Day in June 2021, shortly after Cornbread and Jimmy's first reunion visit,
Jimmy shared a photograph taken at his childhood home in South Minneapolis. He
is playing a drum kit while Cornbread plays organ. Courtesy of James "Jimmy Jam"
Harris III.

THE NEXT TIME I SAW JIMMY was in person a few weeks later in Los Angeles, where we met up to do another interview just outside the city at the studio that he operated with Terry Lewis. Pulling up outside the unmarked warehouse that houses Flyte Tyme, you'd never guess that you were about to walk into the workspace of two of the most prolific and successful songwriters of the past forty years. But once inside, the accolades spoke for themselves. The main room of the studio was a cavernous, two-story-high space that could still just barely contain the rows of awards, gold and platinum records, stacks of keyboards, and miscellaneous memorabilia and instruments collected throughout Jimmy and Terry's celebrated career.

After giving me a tour of the space, Jimmy invited me to sit down across from him at a table and show him all the research I'd gathered about his dad so far. By this point I had filled a three-ring binder with newspaper clippings that were ordered chronologically, starting with the pieces I'd found about Cornbread's mother and grandparents, and dating all the way up to pieces from that year. Together we sat for hours paging through it and talking about his family's roots and his own memories of growing up alongside Cornbread.

By the third hour of our wide-ranging conversation, we turned our attention toward the present moment. When I asked him about what it was like to go see his dad after all that time, Jimmy offered a beautiful reflection.

"It was great," he said, his face relaxing into a peaceful smile. "I thought about something that Terry said one time, back when we used to criticize Prince all the time. When Prince was our boss, and we didn't like a decision Prince made, we would always go, like, 'Yeah, man, if I was doing it, I'd do it like this.' But then when you become the boss, you actually then realize why people are making the decisions they're making; whether you agree with them or not, you can see it from their perspective. I felt that way about being a parent. Because before I was a parent, it was easy for me to say, 'Oh, he abandoned me when I was fourteen or fifteen, whatever age I was. And I never really had any more in-depth thought about it.

"After raising kids, I had a different understanding and a different perspective on what it was that he was experiencing. I was aware of what he was experiencing because I watched the arguments happen. And I watched him, not able to do what he really wanted to do, which was music. And I absolutely understood. So because I had all of those feelings from over the years, I just felt like I wanted him to know that. I just wanted to be able to say that to him. And I felt like that would lift a weight off of him, if he was feeling any sort of weight and any sort of regret about it. So for that reason, it was great."

"And, you know, it's not even that I feel like I need to have this ongoing relationship. But I did feel like we needed to not necessarily bury the hatchet, but just move past that in order to get to anything else that could potentially happen," he continued. "Coming out of it, I just felt like, okay, at least that chapter is clear now. And he knows that I don't harbor any resentment. Now where it goes from there, I don't really know."

Much like the shift I sensed in Cornbread in our most recent visits, getting the hard stuff out of the way seemed to have opened trap doors into long-stowed-away memories in Jimmy's mind. When I asked him how he felt his dad influenced him musically, he jumped at the chance to respond.

"My early tinkling on the piano was all directly related to the way he played. It was all very bluesy," he noted. "And I still have that to this day, although it's not the main thing I do. But I think I had a great appreciation of music because of all the different kinds of music that he played. Like, we would play a country-western song, we'd play a polka song, we'd play a soul song, and he played them all. He was very open to everything."

Jimmy remembered riding in the car with his parents as a kid and getting fidgety with the radio dial, bouncing between the local pop and rock stations to check out all the latest hits. Cornbread didn't just allow him to control the dial but embraced it—ever the generous showman, he would pay attention to what Jimmy liked and incorporate the latest hits into their live act.

"We played 'Dialogue' by Chicago because we heard it on the radio," Jimmy recalled, referring to a song that is sung in a call-and-response style by the band's members Terry Kath and Peter Cetera. When Jimmy and Cornbread played it, it became a conversation between father and son, with Cornbread singing one line from behind his organ and Jimmy responding with a line from behind his drum kit.

"So he had a big influence on my love of music, and how to interpret music and make it your own style," he continued. "It felt as natural for him to do a polka song as a country-western song as a blues song. It all just felt like him. And I love that. I think it made me feel very musically free."

The deeper Jimmy got into his reflection about his dad's influence, the more poignant his memories became. He said his dad was even present in his mind and in his playing when he met one of his most significant early collaborators, a young Prince Rogers Nelson, in the keyboard room at Bryant Junior High School. "I remember when I met Prince for the first time, we were sitting at a keyboard. The first thing I would ever play when I sat at a keyboard would be one of my dad's licks that he would always do— always in the key of C, because that was the basic key. It would always be like a blues-type thing, right? And I remember the first time I did that, I remember Prince sat down and did the identical thing. And it was like we were talking to each other, but we weren't really talking to each other. And it was really cool. That came from my dad, for sure."

When Jimmy said this, it was hard not to mention Prince speaking through his father's influence as well. John L. Nelson, who performed as Prince Rogers, was a locally popular piano player and bandleader who played many of the same venues as Cornbread; though Cornbread says they never shared a bill together, he remembered the Prince Rogers Combo performing around town at the same time he was leading his band the Swing Masters.

It was nightfall by the time I left Flyte Tyme, and after six hours of our talking the batteries in my recorder were nearly worn out. Jimmy walked me out to my car and chatted with me for a few minutes more in the parking lot, giving me a true extended Minnesotan farewell. With my recorder tucked back into my bag, a meaningful afternoon of deep conversation behind us, and my flight back home looming on the horizon, I threw out one last question for him: what if we tried doing a Zoom call when I was at Cornbread's house, so he could do a joint interview with his dad?

"Sure, that'd be cool," he said, offering me a hug and a final goodbye.

Just like Cornbread did every time I left his house, Jimmy stood out in front of his studio and watched me back up my rental car and shift it into drive, smiling and waving to me as I drove away.

Chapter 5

THE CORNBREAD SONG

Cornbread in the morning
Cornbread at night
Cornbread in the forenoon
Everything will be all right
—"The Cornbread Song," Cornbread Harris

A few days after Thanksgiving, with a fresh coat of snow covering the ground outside, I set up my phone on a stand a few feet away from Cornbread's piano, set a Bluetooth speaker next to it to amplify the sound, and opened up a video chat screen.

"We're on something called Zoom," I explained to Cornbread, who watched with wonder as the screen reflected his face back to him. He waved at himself a couple of times, contemplating the speed at which his own image was beamed up into space and back, and let out a little giggle at the strangeness of it all. A moment later, the screen blinked and Jimmy's face suddenly filled the tiny surface. Instead of the typical sunglasses and fedora that Jimmy usually wore during media appearances, he was dressed casually in a black Jam and Lewis baseball cap and black-rimmed eyeglasses.

"Hello!" Jimmy said.

Cornbread gasped. "Hey! How ya doin', champ?" he asked in a high-pitched voice, his excitement barely contained.

Cornbread smiles as he connects for the first time over Zoom with his long-estranged son in late 2021. Courtesy of the author.

"I'm good, how are you?" Jimmy responded enthusiastically.

"I think I'm gonna live, here," Cornbread said, laughing with delight and clapping his hands. After making sure to tell Jimmy that he'd been trying to call him for months, he got right down to business. "I just wanted to make sure that I got ahold of you, because I want you to hear something that you should have your group play. Okay? Listen. Listen to this," Cornbread instructed, shifting into teacher mode. "This is 'Deeper Blues.' I'm a bluesman."

"Okay," Jimmy said, nodding and smiling bashfully. "I know that."

With Jimmy watching him intently, Cornbread did a quick swivel around on his piano bench and launched into the opening progression of "Deeper Blues," hunching one shoulder down toward the low end of the keyboard to accentuate the tension that builds and resolves within the first few chords. Just before the first verse, Cornbread turned back around to face the screen. "What did you think of that?"

"I love it," Jimmy said without a moment's hesitation.

In that first call, with poor cell phone reception threatening to freeze their images in place on the screen, neither Cornbread nor Jimmy knew whether they'd get the chance to talk to each other like this again. I was impressed at just how quickly they jumped from niceties into the "Deeper Blues" and deeper conversations. At times it was easy to forget that I was theoretically supposed to be interviewing them both, as Jimmy had his own questions that he'd been wanting to ask his dad, and it was plenty illuminating just watching them make their way through this pivotal inter-action with one another. But eventually I chimed in with a few things I had been wondering, starting with whether Cornbread gave Jimmy formal piano lessons when he was a kid.

"You couldn't call them lessons, no," Cornbread said.

"That's what I was gonna say, not really lessons. But what he did that I'll always remember—and by the way your grand-son, Max, I taught him this same thing—was just the theory of chords," Jimmy recalled. "Like you had a C chord. And then a major seventh would be the B on top. A seven chord would be the B flat on top. A minor would be dropping the third a half a step. That kind of thing. You absolutely taught me, and I've passed it on to him, too."

"Yeah, yeah. Oh yeah, amen," Cornbread replied.

After jumping around to a few different memories from the past, I gently tossed out another question. What was it like, I asked, to finally see each other again after all these years?

Cornbread answered first. "Oh, man, all I could do was cry and hug. I never got no addresses. No names. No nothing. Man, after he left it was, like, 'Well, who was that guy?' No, no, not quite that bad. Not quite that bad," he said, giggling and punctuating his thoughts with a clap. "Man, the daycare people were thrilled to see a big star come to the place."

"I don't know about a big star," Jimmy said shyly, almost under his breath.

"Well, that's what they think, okay? That's what the daycare people thought," Cornbread retorted. "I could have told 'em he ain't nobody," he added, a wry smile stretching across his face.

"I thought it was great," Jimmy added. "And you could tell your circle of people all really cared about you. It was good to see. You still go there a couple times a week?"

"Yes I do, Mondays and Wednesdays," Cornbread said, adding that he was also playing a couple of gigs that kept him busy the rest of the week. Around the time we first video-chatted with Jimmy in the fall of 2021, Covid restrictions had started easing in the Twin Cities and Cornbread had started a Sunday evening residency at Palmer's Bar, a longtime favorite spot near the West Bank in Minneapolis, close to the University of Minnesota. The increased show activity clearly energized him. "All you gotta do is ask me. 'Cornbread, you want to play?' 'Yep,'" he said. "Music is number one. Number one. There's nothing I like better except God. That's it."

"Music, to me, is the way God speaks to us," Jimmy opined. "It's the language of God."

"Oh yeah. That 'devil's music' thing came from people who were jealous," Cornbread added. "They just couldn't stand it. 'You're playing the devil's music.' No, I'm not! I'm playing God's music!"

Jimmy nodded and rested his chin on his hand. "Well, to me music is virtual time travel. Because, you know, if I just named any random date and said, 'What were you doing on that day?' you could probably piece it together like, 'Oh, I might have been living here. I might have been doing that.' But if I play a song from that date, every memory comes back."

"Oh, yeah," Cornbread confirmed.

"Which means that music is the thing that unlocks it. That's divine," Jimmy added.

"Oh, man. Music has unlocked a whole lot of stuff here, for

me and you," Cornbread said, pointing at Jimmy's image on the screen and nodding. "Yes, it has."

By the end of that first Zoom call, Cornbread had not only had the opportunity to play several songs for Jimmy and discover new connection points in their lives, but he also got to meet his granddaughter, Bella, and his grandson, Tyler, and to say hello to Max again, smiling ear to ear as they all took turns crowding behind Jimmy on the screen. An hour flew by in what felt like a few minutes, and neither Jimmy nor Cornbread was eager to end the call.

Much to our surprise, before we disconnected Jimmy suggested that we chat again the following week, and that we make a plan to connect regularly in the future. Once the call was over, Cornbread looked stunned.

"Oh, wow," Cornbread said, resting his back against his piano keys. "Wow."

For the first time in nearly fifty years, Jimmy and Cornbread started talking regularly on those Tuesday afternoon Zoom calls as I sat quietly by and took notes about their latest revelations. Things didn't always go smoothly; try as I might to bring the right technology to Cornbread's house, those first few calls would often be interrupted by freezing screens and robotic, garbled sound. But the three of us persevered.

It didn't take long for a more complete picture of Jimmy's childhood—and Cornbread's life in the '60s and '70s—to come into view. As we settled into our collaborative chats, I saw that this was the earliest period in Cornbread's life where I could invite another voice in to share their first-person recollections, and it was illuminating to gain a better sense of what he was like as both a father and a musician who was at that point already a couple of decades into his performance career.

Throughout this period of his life, music was always a side hustle and passion project for Cornbread. He held down a full-time day job at American Hoist and Derrick in St. Paul and later at another foundry in Minneapolis, Grease & Hydraulics, and would pick up additional odd jobs to help make ends meet. From an early age, Jimmy remembered Cornbread and his mother, Bertha, striving to make his childhood special despite their somewhat limited means.

Jimmy's first mention in a newspaper occurred in June 1962 when he turned three years old. The *Minneapolis Spokesman*, where Bertha worked part-time, offered a vignette of the day: "Balloons floating gently through the air, fiesta straw hats, decorations of pink, blue, and white individual cup cakes and candles, gifts, and you've guessed it . . . someone is having a party. Master Jimmy Harris, son of Mr. and Mrs. James S. Harris, 4100 Portland Ave. S., celebrated his third birthday Wednesday, June 6, with a few of his little friends."

Two years later, his fifth birthday party was also documented, and it was noted that "Jimmy Harris . . . was the center of attraction" and that "clever little clowns" were the theme of the party's decor.

"Wow," Jimmy said when I showed him the clippings. "Reading those columns was the Instagram of today."

In addition to the elaborate birthday parties, Jimmy remembered his dad going above and beyond to make Christmases memorable. "Christmastime, he worked at Sears in the toys department. Whenever something came back to the store that was damaged, he would fix it, and then it would be under the tree. He'd take, like, three Hot Wheel tracks that were missing parts or whatever, and then I'd wake up on Christmas morning and there'd be this huge Hot Wheels track. I never felt like I was poor, because I never felt like I was lacking anything. And I didn't know he couldn't afford them, or that he was just taking all the spare pieces that nobody was using and putting it together."

Jimmy recalled that his dad kept a workroom in their family home that was stocked with musical instruments, including a piano and an electronic Wurlitzer, and a bench full of tools. It was at that workbench that Cornbread first constructed what became a constant staple of his live setup, and something he wore whether he was playing piano alone in the corner of a bar or with his band in front of hundreds: a thick metal hanger that had been carefully bent to hang around his neck and hold his microphone right in front of his mouth.

"I remember when he did it. I thought, well, wow, that's genius," Jimmy said. "I always thought, somebody is going to actually come up with a real version of that. But he always stuck with the hanger. And the thing was, it used to drive my mom crazy. She thought it was so tacky," he added, laughing. "He'd always tinker around."

Cornbread loved to talk about his homemade mic holder. "All these mics are on stands and it's in your face, and you've got to lean over to get to the microphone. I'm thinking, 'This isn't working.' I know they had them fancy ones you could buy and pin on yourself, with these little wires going up to the ears and everything. But, you know, all these places *have* microphones," he explained. "So I got the coat hanger, put it on, bent it all kinds of ways. I have to have a heavy-duty coat hanger, 'cause most of those microphones are pretty heavy. You get pliers, make sure it's good and solid. That's my kind of thing."

Another element of Cornbread's live set that began back in the '60s was his trademark number "The Cornbread Song," which gave him his longtime stage name. "The song became kind of popular, and then people expected me to play that song whenever I played anywhere," he said. "So somewhere along the line they started calling me Cornbread, like my song. Like Prince got the name from his father's band? My name came from the song I wrote."

Cornbread loved to tell this story about how he got his name, and he would often launch into the opening lines of the song to illustrate his point:

Cornbread in the morning
Cornbread every night
Cornbread in the forenoon
Everything will be all right

93

I said cornbread
I said cornbread
I said cornbread, I love the good cornbread

"And then you get the rhythm going, and I've got lists of stuff. Food kinda stuff and cornbread. People's jobs and cornbread. Different religions and cornbread," he explained. The song did indeed include several running lists of things that pair well with cornbread, starting with classic Southern Black food staples like collard greens and chitlins, then moving on to describe all the different kinds of people, from Episcopalians to Muslims to truck drivers, sales people, and redheads, who enjoyed the food. By the end, you get the message: cornbread is for everyone.

Cornbread couldn't quite remember when he first came up with his personal anthem. To both of our surprise, I found a mention of his nickname dating as early as January 28, 1965, when his band the Swingsters, Inc. was listed in an item about the Credjafawn Social Club's charity dance at the Prom Center; the *Minneapolis Spokesman*'s preview of the event noted that the band would be "held together by Jimmy (Cornbread) Harris, piano and electronic wurlitzer."

After leaving the Augie Garcia group in the mid-'50s, Cornbread had restarted his band the Swing Masters, and it went through several iterations in the following decade. In 1964, the band was advertised as the Swing Masters (Jim Harris & His 9 Piece Orchestra), but by the following year it had morphed into the five-piece Swingsters, Inc., with Cornbread's Augie Garcia bandmate Willy Brown on alto and tenor sax, Mel Carter on trumpet, Joel Beal on drums, and Commodore Lark on bass.

"If you don't dance," the article about their Credjafawn fundraiser gig noted, "you can get your donation's worth by just hearing these jazz stars work out!"

In addition to leading a group, Cornbread was also performing on his own. Somehow between holding down his day job at the foundry and picking up other odd jobs, he also went through stints performing weekly and sometimes nightly residencies. In 1963, an ad for downtown bar and restaurant Herman's beckoned patrons to "Swing with Jimmy Harris at the Piano Pallette—Nitely," promising the sound of "Mellow New Orlean's rhythms" [*sic*]. By 1966, another ad in the *Minneapolis Morning Tribune* advertised a Sunday evening residency at the Gaslight featuring "Jimmy Harris the Swingmaster." Remarkably, his weekly set would start at 4 p.m. and go for more than six hours until the Gaslight closed at 10:30 p.m.—a testament to just how many songs Cornbread had in his repertoire by this point in his career as an entertainer.

The next year, in 1967, Cornbread was billing himself as the Jimmy Harris Trio and continued to play neighborhood events, fundraisers, and dances, including a well-attended party for the Fezzan Temple Shriners that earned him another mention in the *Spokesman.* His reputation in the Twin Cities as a respected bandleader helped him to connect with all the best jazz and blues players of the day, and by the end of the '60s he was also sitting in with nationally revered players like Mojo Buford and Lazy Bill Lucas in addition to leading his own group.

Jimmy Jam's first memory of seeing his dad play occurred around the end of the 1960s when Cornbread connected with Charlie Clarke, a saxophonist and music teacher for junior high students in Minneapolis Public

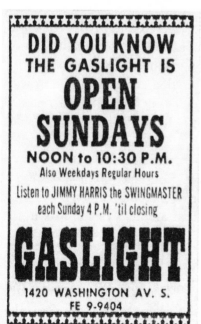

DID YOU KNOW
THE GASLIGHT IS
OPEN
SUNDAYS
NOON to 10:30 P.M.
Also Weekdays Regular Hours
Listen to JIMMY HARRIS the SWINGMASTER
each Sunday 4 P.M. 'til closing
GASLIGHT
1420 WASHINGTON AV. S.
FE 9-9404

An advertisement in the *Minneapolis Tribune* on March 13, 1966, for one of the many house gigs Cornbread (billed as Jimmy Harris the Swingmaster) played in the 1960s.

Before he was known as Cornbread, an early advertisement in the *Minneapolis Morning Tribune,* dated October 24, 1963, promised "Mellow New Orlean's Rhythms" from house pianist Jimmy Harris, who held down a nightly residency at Herman's in downtown Minneapolis.

Schools, and joined his horn-heavy band the Paramounts. As with many memories from Jimmy's childhood, the thing he remembers most is the music; he knows that at one of the rehearsals he attended with his dad, Charlie Clarke and the Paramounts were learning the then-new song "Super Bad" by James Brown, so he guesses it would have been around 1970. (The three-part single was released on October 2, 1970.)

Jimmy guessed that it was through Charlie Clarke that his dad ended up taking part in the watershed recording session with James Bonner in 1970. The single "Don't Rush It" was released in June 1971 on local imprint BPL Records and had a serious enough push that it was mentioned in an ad in *Billboard* magazine that month. While we know that Cornbread wasn't able to go on tour with James Bonner to support the single, Jimmy doesn't recall (and there is little information available to indicate) whether the tour happened or the song had any legs beyond its initial warm reception.

IT'S AN UNDERSTATEMENT to note that the 1960s dramatically shifted the musical landscape in the Twin Cities, when an explosion of young garage rock bands, folk songwriters, funk groups,

and blues-rock-loving hippies drowned out the previous generation's big band and swing bands. After evolving his Swingmasters
group through several smaller and smaller iterations, Cornbread
finally settled into a trio format that he would stick with through
the next decade. Huckleberry Finn, Cornbread and Friends,
sometimes billed as Huckleberry Finn, Cornbread and a Friend,
would become Cornbread's prevailing focus musically, and the
group would provide an entry point for his son Jimmy to get onstage with him.

The first name in the group, Huckleberry Finn, was a reference to a childhood nickname that Cornbread picked up as
he was running to catch the bus to summer camp at the Hallie Q. Brown Community Center in Rondo. "My grandparents
had dressed me up like an old person with a stick and a sack and
a straw hat," he recalled, guessing he would have been about ten
years old at the time. "And here I'm coming down the street toward the bus, I'm running a little late, and some kid yelled out of
the bus, 'Here comes Huckleberry Finn!' They must have been
studying it in school or something, and this was on his young
mind. So in St. Paul they know me as Huck."

When Cornbread first told this story to me, I chuckled at
the notion that his trio included two different references to himself. In the early '70s, when Huckleberry Finn, Cornbread and
Friends got going, the trio was anchored by Cornbread on Farfisa
organ and his close collaborator Vernon Coffee on guitar. The
"Friend" in the group was a rotating cast of different drummers,
none of whom seemed to stick around for long.

Around the time that Jimmy and Cornbread first reunited,
Jimmy started mentioning his dad in interviews that he was
doing; in the spring of 2020, he had told the story about how he
ended up playing in Huckleberry Finn, Cornbread and Friends to
Questlove for his podcast *Questlove Supreme*. "They could never
keep a drummer. So every week there'd be, like, a different drummer," Jimmy recalled. "So eventually there was a gig and the
drummer didn't show up, and my mom said, 'Why don't you let

Cornbread *(center)* with guitarist Vernon Coffee and drummer Dan Welch in the publicity photo for the Huckleberry Finn, Cornbread and Friends Trio. Cornbread is playing the Farfisa organ that Jimmy Jam and Terry Lewis "borrowed" for their first-ever gig together in the summer of 1973. Courtesy of the Minnesota Historical Society.

Jimmy play a set? He knows all your songs. He's been watching you play for all this time.' So I did. I sat in, I did one set with him and stuff and everybody liked it, crowd liked it, okay. So couple weeks later, same thing. So Coffee, the guitar player said, 'Hey Jim, why don't you let your son go ahead and play? He knows the show, why don't you let him play?' After the end of that gig,

Coffee said to my dad, 'Why don't you just let your son play, man? We don't have to keep finding drummers, you know.' So my dad said, 'Okay, cool, we'll let you play. You're our drummer.' So my mom said, 'How much are you going to pay him?' She became my agent real quick. And then my dad said, 'Oh you know, I'll throw him out a little something something.' And she said, 'Oh no, you're going to pay him just like you'd pay any drummer that you pay.' And that was the start of my gigging."

Jimmy thinks he was eleven or twelve years old when he joined his dad's group and started gigging professionally. He remembers they learned how to perform the Chicago song "Dialogue" (released on *Chicago V* on July 12, 1972) and listened to Barry White's "I'm Gonna Love You Just a Little More, Baby" (released in April 1973) on the drive to gigs at the Surfside on Lake Minnetonka with his dad. And he recalls he was still playing with his dad's group in the summer of 1973 when he met Terry Lewis at the Upward Bound summer program at the University of Minnesota—a friendship that was solidified when the two of them caught a ride to another Lake Minnetonka supper club, the Caribbean Club, to "borrow" Cornbread's Farfisa so they could play their first gig together at the program's graduation party.

Cornbread let out a delighted squeal when Jimmy regaled him with the story of stealing his organ all those years ago. Cornbread doesn't remember whatever happened to that Farfisa, but they were both delighted to learn that the organ was captured for posterity in the publicity photo for Huckleberry Finn, Cornbread and Friends, which is now part of the archives at the Minnesota Historical Society. The photograph features Cornbread standing behind the organ, Vernon Coffee holding an electric guitar, and the drummer who eventually replaced Jimmy and remained in the group throughout the rest of the 1970s, Dan Welch, seated behind the kit.

Prior to his reconciliation with Jimmy, Cornbread would often refer to that summer of 1973, when Jimmy met Terry, in the same way: that was the summer that Jimmy began to pull away and to head down his own path in music—and in life. Once Cornbread and Jimmy started talking, however, we learned more about the events that occurred in this pivotal period in both of their lives, and how their stories continued to intertwine throughout the mid-1970s.

It would take several years for Terry Lewis to officially incorporate Jimmy into his group Flyte Tyme. That summer, as Jimmy's horizons expanded through the Upward Bound program and gigs with his dad, he started playing in other bands and refining his own sound—but they weren't funk bands on the North Side. They were blues-rock bands filled with white teenagers from the west metro suburb of Robbinsdale, Minnesota. Cornbread would even occasionally sit in with the groups.

AFTER THE THREE OF US had been connecting for regular Zoom calls for a few months, Jimmy started texting me little snippets of things he suddenly remembered: band names, venues, people, hit songs that were on the radio when his career first began to take shape. Eventually he and I were able to put together a rough time line and establish that his first band after playing with Huckleberry Finn, Cornbread and Friends was the teenaged band Tanglefoot. Learning about Tanglefoot provided another fascinating entry point into Cornbread's story in this era. Many of the members were still around and willing to chat with me about these nascent days, and some even still lived in the Twin Cities. (Unfortunately, Cornbread's bandmates Vernon Coffee and Dan Welch had both passed away by the time we started working on this book.)

I even tracked down Tanglefoot's manager, who was a few years older than the rest of the group and who had a hand in bringing Jimmy into their orbit. "We were young," remembered Tanglefoot's Ron Tracy, who now runs a guitar repair shop in St. Paul. "And we were playing professionally—we were playing clubs, even though we shouldn't have been."

The early '70s teen band Tanglefoot in the basement of the Tempo Bar on Lake Street in Minneapolis: bandleader Gary Lickness, keys and sax player Jimmy Harris, bassist John Tracy, and guitarist Ron Tracy (standing), with vocalist Katie Lee Andersen and drummer Tom Lickness (seated). Photograph courtesy of Katie Lee Andersen.

As Ron told it, Tanglefoot was started by the aspiring rock star Gary Lickness and his girlfriend, Katie Lee, who were upper-class students at Robbinsdale High School. Gary had already had a couple of other successful groups and had even recorded a 45 single with his band the Glass Opening, "I'm on Your Prey," b/w "My Heart Is Heavy," copies of which are still floating around on Discogs. Ron thinks Tanglefoot got going in 1972, when he was only a freshman in high school and his younger brother John was in the eighth grade; the band was rounded out by Gary's younger brother Tom, who was also a freshman then, on drums.

The band was managed by Lynn Preston, who was in his mid-twenties and had gotten his start in the music business working with country artists at Sound 80 with the studio's owner, Herb Pilhofer. Lynn told me that as the band was changing over from the Glass Opening to Tanglefoot, they put the word out that they needed a new keyboardist. They got word from someone from the music shop B Sharp Music, which was something of a hot spot for teen bands and garage rock musicians in the '60s and '70s, that there was a young kid hanging out there who could really play. One thing led to another and eventually Lynn got a phone number and invited the young whiz kid to come sit in with the band.

"I called Cornbread, actually, and said that we'd like to set up a rehearsal and have Jimmy come up and sit in," Lynn recalled. "I think it was at Robbinsdale Elementary School. It was up in that area. And I remember it was kind of funny, because I was expecting a little kid to come in—and Jimmy has never been little. He was taller than me. And so he came to the rehearsal and came up to me with that big smile, and I asked him, 'Did you bring your brother?' He said, 'No, *I'm* Jimmy!'"

By the end of the rehearsal that day, it was clear that Jimmy was going to be the newest member of Tanglefoot. But before he left, he told Lynn that he should call his parents to talk over the details, since he was only a junior high student at the time.

"So I called, and Cornbread and his wife, Bertha, asked me over to dinner. So I went over to dinner at his place," Lynn continued. "The thing I remember about Cornbread at that meeting was he told me his parents had died when he was young. And my mother died when I was five years old. So we kind of related there. He said he was raised by his grandparents, but he kind of had three or four other places, I think, before he landed at his grandparents' place. And I said, well, I was raised by my grandparents,

Jimmy Harris plays saxophone with his first band, Tanglefoot, in the early '70s. Photograph courtesy of Katie Lee Andersen.

too. We had a good discussion. And Jimmy joined the band. And he was very good. I mean, he was good from the beginning."

"Jimmy was a pretty cool guy," recalls John Tracy. "He played keyboards, and he played them well. And that was key at that time, you know, because we're all trying to improve ourselves and be the best musicians we can, and when you're playing with other good musicians it tends to make you better. And he was a showman back then."

Lynn remembered Jimmy's mother being very involved in the

band's progress. "Cornbread, he played a lot with his own band, so I don't remember him coming to a lot of the places we played. But Bertha, she would call me after each time we played. She'd call and wonder how everything went." After a couple of months, she called up Lynn and asked him to stop by for lunch. "She said, 'I'd like to ask you a very personal question,'" Lynn recalled. "She said, 'We don't feel very comfortable going to a lot of the clubs, so I'd like you to watch out for Jimmy.'"

At this time, Cornbread was gigging regularly at places all throughout the Twin Cities, but there was still a strong bias and discrimination against Black musicians playing certain kinds of clubs. Tanglefoot was booked to play all the hottest spots in the early '70s, including Duffy's in South Minneapolis, Duff's downtown, and a sprawling venue called Country Dam on the Apple River in Wisconsin, and they performed to almost exclusively white audiences. Because all the members were so young, Lynn remembers shielding them from some of the more complex realities of navigating the club scene at the time.

"Jimmy being a Black kid, some of the people were not prejudiced but squeamish, I would say, especially since they were all kids. I remember one time I was with the manager sitting in Duffy's, waiting to sign our contract. And he said, 'Well, you have a Black kid.' And I said, 'Yeah, so? He's a really good player, and he's a big part of our band.' And he said, 'The only thing is, some people don't want Black guys hanging around with white girls.' And I said, 'Well, the times are changing.' And at that time, Jimmy comes in the door, 'Hey, Lynn!' He waves and smiles, and here he's holding hands with his white girlfriend. I said, 'See? Times are changing!'"

"I mean, we were like fourteen, fifteen years old, and we were playing in bars where we weren't supposed to be," remembers John Tracy. "We were kind of Jimmy's ride. So we'd go get him and bring him to everything, and he spent some nights at our house. And that was fun. Because, you know, all we did was just goof off and play music and have fun. We were your typical kids."

Eventually Tanglefoot got a house gig at a venue called the Tempo on East Lake Street in a building that would later become the Blue Nile. Cornbread would occasionally come by and sit in with the band at the Tempo, which left a strong impression on all of the young members.

"I vividly remember Jimmy's dad," said Tanglefoot's lead singer Katie Lee Andersen. "He'd get up with us on occasion and play two songs that stand out: he'd do 'Cornbread in the Morning, Cornbread,'" she continued, breaking into song. "And then it was 'Pink Champagne That Stole My Gal from Me.' And I mean, even as a high school kid, you could recognize that talent in both of them. You know, it was a step above all the rest. They were really a wonderful addition to our musical life. And now I recognize that it was really quite an honor to have him get up and play with us."

"We were invited to go see Cornbread play," Ron Tracy recalled. "Our parents had to chaperone us. And I remember him sitting in with us and playing 'Cornbread.' It was a big deal. I don't know how Jimmy felt about that. But it was a big deal for everybody else."

By the mid-1970s Tanglefoot's leader Gary Lickness and singer Katie Lee left the band, and the group evolved into Skye, mixing original tunes in with the blues and rock songs they'd worked up by bands like Chicago and Grand Funk Railroad. Brothers John and Ron Tracy even had an opportunity to audition for Jimmy's next group, which turned out to be the Philadelphia Soul–inspired Mind and Matter, but they decided that they would rather stick with the blues sound. "That was a mistake, as far as I'm concerned," John Tracy said, chuckling. "I should have stuck with him. But we were musicians, and we all go our own ways and do our own music. And that's when he started up with The Time and went that direction and took off—it went crazy."

Katie Lee said that after leaving the band she lost track of Jimmy and had no idea that he ended up pursuing a career in music. It wasn't until she was on an airplane in the early 2000s

A young Jimmy Harris perched behind a stack of gear *(top right)* in this photograph of the mid-'70s teen band Skye, which also included Michael Laffey on vocals, Dave Johansen on guitar, Dan Borden on drums, and Ron Tracy on guitar *(standing)*, along with bassist John Tracy and roadie John Bunda *(seated)*. Photograph courtesy of Ronald Lee Tracy.

and randomly spotted a Northwest Airlines *World Traveler* magazine cover story about Jam and Lewis that she finally connected the dots: he had become Jimmy Jam. "I was flying home from a business trip and the magazine talked about Jimmy Jam Harris. And I looked, and I thought, that's our Jimmy!"

THERE'S NO QUESTION that things got complicated between Cornbread and Bertha, and between Cornbread and Jimmy, and that what transpired through the rest of the 1970s gave them plenty of reason to build up hard feelings toward one another. As they reconciled, it became clear that trying to retrace the events around Cornbread and Bertha's divorce wasn't only unnecessary but nearly impossible; Bertha passed away in 1990, and Cornbread's memories about their dissolution had long since faded away. What had remained, and what only became clearer the more we all connected and researched and reminisced, was that he had most certainly played a significant role in Jimmy's early musical development, and that the lessons he taught him had endured.

"That's a real history," Cornbread said one day, after listening to me regale him with stories about the lifelong impression he had made on the young musicians who played with Jimmy in Tanglefoot. "When they say the Minneapolis Sound, before Prince and Jimmy Jam and them guys, *we* were making music. And we're the foundation underneath. A good solid foundation, by the way." As he spoke, Cornbread's eyes started to tear up. "I keep being amazed that I am one of the cornerstones, the foundations of the Minneapolis Sound. I keep repeating this over and over: amazing, amazing, amazing."

With that, he turned to his piano and launched into his song "Lesson," which he wrote decades ago and had been trying to sing to Jimmy ever since. Unlike the song "Cool Rider," which rollicks along to a jump beat, "Lesson" was a ballad that Cornbread played extra softly on the piano, singing so quietly that his voice was almost a whisper:

> Listen to another man
> Even though you think he's wrong
> Diplomacy is something grand
> You may sing a different song
> There's no tit for tat
> There's no time for that
> This is a lesson to my son
>
> James, you must do everything you can
> Building up the spirit in yourself
> To help your fellow man
> There's no tit for tat
> There's no room for that
> Da da da da da

Be honest and forgiving
Very hard to do
Bring satisfaction and living
That comes to quite a few
Never hold your head so high
You fail to see another
Good things will pass you by
We are one another
This is a lesson to my son

Sometimes reconciliation looks like two people trying to under-stand each other's emotions or rehash the reasons their relation-ship faded away. It was not lost on me that for Jimmy and Corn-bread, part of their journey was to just get to a point where they could cut through the din and really see and hear each other. "My vision's down, my hearing's down, but my spirits are up," Corn-bread would joke as he squinted to make out his son's silhouette on the tiny iPhone screen.

As the holidays approached, Jimmy told me to look out for a package he was sending our way. A few days later, a FedEx box filled with meticulously wrapped presents arrived for Cornbread, and on the Tuesday between Christmas and New Year's we got on a Zoom call with Jimmy, and Cornbread slowly, carefully un-wrapped each one. Inside was a new iPhone, a phone case, a new iPad, and what would become one of Cornbread's prized posses-sions: an elaborate, trifold Christmas card featuring portraits of Jimmy, Lisa, and their three children.

Cornbread held the card up proudly and showed it to me. "Outstanding," he said. "And he looks like a proud papa, too, don't he? 'Look what I fostered.' Go ahead with your bad self," he said, turning to address Jimmy on the screen. "This is going on my wall. These are my grandchildren!"

Cornbread tenderly folded up each scrap of wrapping paper and ribbon and tucked them away to be treasured and saved. As he pored over his many gifts, Jimmy's family came into view and crowded around the screen to wish Cornbread a Merry Christmas.

"Oh man, this is so wonderful," Cornbread gushed, waving at the screen proudly. "This is more than merry. I mean, the humans only have a few words to discuss something really wonderful— and whatever they are, they don't match up to this."

When we got off the Zoom call, Cornbread seemed hesitant to let me leave. I could tell that he had spent most of the Christmas weekend in a quiet house and was eager to socialize with company. ("I just love this fraternizing," he would often say to me, appearing more energized the longer our conversations wore on.) For the first time in the six months I had been visiting him, Cornbread stood up from his piano bench and asked me to follow him into the kitchen so he could show me another gift that his nephew, Renee, had given him for Christmas. He slowly shuffled out of the dining room and around the corner toward his cupboards, then opened up one of the cabinet doors and pointed up at the shelf at an extra large container of Taster's Choice instant coffee—the kind of oversized plastic jug you might buy at a bulk superstore, which would surely last him for months.

"Like I said, I'm a blessed dude! I can't shake it," Cornbread told me, beaming proudly. For all the expensive gifts he'd just received from his son, it was clear that this present meant just as much, if not more, to him. He reached up and tenderly grabbed it off the shelf and lowered it to the kitchen counter.

"Let me be the chef, cook," he joked. "I'm a really good cook. I can burn water."

He took two mugs out of a drying rack and carefully rinsed out each one, then filled them with water and asked me to help him read the directions off the side of the instant coffee jar. Together we scooped a heaping teaspoon of coffee into each cup and then I popped open the door of the microwave so he could lift each one and place it inside. "Go, Cornbread, go," he said under his breath, egging himself on as he puttered around the kitchen and gathered up sugar packets and spoons for us both.

As we stood in the kitchen and sipped our coffee, Cornbread sighed and smiled. "A Christmas gift, isn't that something? From

Renee, Renee and Kathy," he said, referring to his nephew and his nephew's wife. "They are my relatives. Renee is my sister's child."

"He used to be your drummer at Nikki's Cafe, right?" I asked.

"He did a little drumming, yeah," Cornbread said, smiling at the fact that I had familiarized myself with his family tree. "He still likes to make a little noise once in a while. Sometimes he comes over here and I play the piano and he puts two sticks together." Cornbread stopped to take another sip. "I was telling Renee, too, about people giving. He gave me that," he said, pointing to the coffee jar. "That's small compared to what Jimmy gave me, and I appreciate it just as much." His mind wandered toward a story from his Bible studies about how God doesn't judge people for how much they give to the church, whether it's only a few cents or millions of dollars—it's the act of giving that actually holds value.

"You know," I offered, "Jimmy asked me if the two of you had things in common, and I said that you both like to tell stories that have lessons in them. He does that, too."

"Yeah?" Cornbread said, grinning. "See, this all reflects back on me, by him being such a great, wonderful guy," he enthused. "Well, I'm glad I was able to raise a child that came out okay. I can't take a lot of the blame for it, but God was good to me again. You and him both, you're a big part of my blessings. So no matter how it all went, with us not speaking for twenty-four years and all that stuff? That's all just water under the bridge."

"Well I think it's a beautiful story," I replied. "If you guys can come back together after that much time, then I think anyone should be able to figure it out and get back together."

Cornbread loved the idea that his story might inspire someone else; we talked about it often. "Come and see my guy; he'll do for you like he's been doing for me," Cornbread said, turning his attention back to God. "Ninety-four years he took care of me, and I think for however many days I got left, he'll be taking care of me that whole time, too. Like I tell 'em, I'm shooting for 125 years. How old are you?"

"I'm thirty-eight," I said.

"I'm ninety-four. So when I'm 125, how old will you be?"

"I'll be . . . sixty-nine," I said, doing the math in my head.

"That's a good number," he assured me. "You'll only be just getting started."

I sipped my coffee slowly, savoring it even as it cooled, and made a point to take a mental snapshot of us standing there together in that kitchen. Outside, the sun had set and the houses down the street were all lit up with holiday lights. Over our two mugs of instant coffee, Cornbread had taught me a lesson about what his belief in God was really all about: it was about remaining grateful for all that he had been given in life, and expressing that gratitude to God and everyone he encountered each day in order to keep the blessings flowing among himself, his community, and the spiritual universe.

To be honest, before I got to know Cornbread I hadn't thought much about God or religion since my Sunday school days. But I felt that something outside my control had guided me into Cornbread's life—and that if he saw me as one of his blessings, I knew that he was most certainly one of mine. The music, the stories, and the camaraderie we shared gave me something to believe in and to feel thankful about that holiday season. And the more we hung out, the more I got the sense that I might be a blessed dude, too.

Chapter 6

TELL ME I'M YOUR MAN

Tell me you know my plan
Tell me you understand
You make me very happy, baby
Tell me I'm your man
—"Tell Me I'm Your Man," Cornbread Harris

The winter months were hard on everyone in Minnesota
that year, including Cornbread and me. As Covid numbers began to rise again, the virus swept through my household
in January 2022, forcing me to stop visiting Cornbread for a few
weeks—which after visiting him weekly for months suddenly felt
like an eternity. At the same time, venues started enforcing restrictions again, canceling some shows and limiting the attendance at
others to try to slow the spread of illness.

Even when we couldn't be together, I would call Cornbread
every Tuesday afternoon to check in and see how he was doing.
Remarkably, even when the pandemic was raging and he was trav-
eling between his house, his daycare center, Palmer's, and other
venues, he never caught Covid. Still, I could hear the sound of
fatigue in his voice as we were all forced to slow down again.

"My connections are falling by the wayside, my gigs are falling
by the wayside. I don't know," Cornbread said, sighing. "Maybe
this and maybe that, and could be. That's the standard conversation now."

"I know, we're all just trying to get through it," I replied. "I'm sorry you can't go out and play your gigs. I know that's hard."

"It is, it really is. Like I say, what day is it? I get up in the morning, I put on the clothes, I sit around in the clothes all day, and in the evening I take 'em off and go to bed. That's really living an exciting life, I guess you could call it," he said, chuckling. "So yeah, I get on the phone and I don't know what to say."

"That's okay, you don't have to say anything. I just wanted to make sure you're okay," I assured him.

"I'm still a blessed dude, though," he added.

"Yes, you are."

"Yes, I am, yes, I am. To be able to stand up face to face against that doggone thing and laugh and smile, and understand that hey, you've been very, very blessed to not have it, and it's causing havoc with your schedule and all that, but you still don't have that virus. God's still in the blessing business," he said. "My buddy's got me in his hand."

While Cornbread and I were apart, I started thinking about different ways I could dig into the lesser-documented parts of his life. Cornbread didn't remember very much about the period between when he left his marriage to Bertha in the late '70s and when he emerged triumphantly in the early '90s as a beloved figure at the buzzy Warehouse District bar Nikki's Cafe. The '80s, as a whole, were unquestionably difficult for him; it seemed possible that there were pieces of this period that he chose to forget long before the effects of aging came along to wipe the slate clean.

What I was able to turn up in public records painted a stark picture of a tumultuous time in Cornbread's personal life. Shortly after his divorce from Bertha was finalized he married Carol Ann Parsons, a drummer he had hired to play with him in Huckleberry, Cornbread and Friends and who was in her early twenties when they got together in 1980. Together they welcomed Cornbread's youngest daughter, Jennifer, in July 1982, but two and a half years later Carol and Jennifer moved out, and Cornbread was divorced again. He got married a fourth time to Roberta Foster

Cornbread performs at various venues in the early 1980s. Courtesy of the Harris family.

Bryant in 1985, then divorced and quickly got married to his current wife, Sabreen Hasan, in 1994. Aside from a few months here and there, Cornbread had been married continuously to different women for most of his adult life.

"There it is, in black-and-white, right down the front. Man," Cornbread said, listening intently as I listed off his various marriage and divorce dates. "I was wondering why I didn't go chasing around much. Because that's about all the ladies I ever bothered with!"

Ever the philosophical thinker, Cornbread sat for a while soaking in all I'd just told him. "Pert near everything in my life that got me this far has been a blessing," he concluded. "I mean all the divorces, the whole thing, as you go through the story to now? I don't know many ninety-four-year-olds that got it as good as me."

That winter I also met up with Cornbread's daughter Jennifer to learn more about her memories of their family. Much like Jimmy, she and Cornbread shared a lot of common traits even though they were apart for much of her early childhood: they both navigate the world with emotional openness and warmth, and they have no trouble shifting quickly between small talk and issues of the heart. They are both quick to crack a joke, especially when discussing more serious topics, and they love to tease each other relentlessly.

"My father is a player," Jennifer told me bluntly, a mischievous twinkle in her eye. "I'm, like, so *that's* where I get it from. But I try not to use my powers."

Jennifer and I met up for brunch to go over the research I'd accumulated, including the marriage records throughout Cornbread's life. "I thought he was married even more times than this," she said, paging through the files. "But you see how quick his marriages were. He's never been alone, and he never will be alone. I think that stems from childhood things, you know, going from place to place, being in an orphanage. And he'll admit it."

Because Jennifer was so young when her parents divorced, she doesn't remember much of anything about Cornbread and Carol together. "They had a tumultuous relationship," she noted, summarizing what she'd gleaned from them both over the years. "I mean, it just

Cornbread with his daughter Jennifer Harris, in the mid-1990s. Courtesy of Cornbread Harris.

116

wasn't a healthy relationship, and it was time for it to end. And so he got ghosted."

The end of his marriage to Carol is the part that stuck with Cornbread, too. After asking him about Carol a few times over a few different weeks, a painful memory emerged. "I took her into my band to play the drums," he recalled. "And that was the wrong thing to do. Some fella came up and started praising her about how good a drummer she was. And he was a rich guy, and I'm floundering trying to make a living. And he told her how good she could have it if she would go with him. And she went with him. Left a note on the counter, right there," he said, gesturing toward the kitchen. "Talking about that she couldn't be messing with somebody in rag tags."

When I recounted this story to Jennifer, she pointed out that Cornbread had written a song inspired by this same anecdote, titled "Cryin' All Alone":

Well she left a note
From this note I quote:
Well, you brought home those clothes in a Goodwill bag
I said, what's the matter, baby?
She said, I ain't gonna have my kids in no rag tags
Ah yes, money, money was the cause
Oh yeah, you gold diggers just stand up in applause
We could have made it, mama, on a whole lot less
And we would have had a little love nest

I should cry, know I should
But I know it wouldn't do me no damn good
'Cause I'd be sittin' here cryin' all alone

Reflecting on the song, Jennifer wondered whether the line might have blurred between fact and fiction in this retelling. What she did know for certain is that her parents were both passionate about music, which was also passed down to her. "My mom is very musical, she's always been a singer," Jennifer said. "So that definitely inspired me to do the same thing growing up."

Jennifer says she spent her early childhood living with her mother and stepfather and then returned to live with Cornbread as a preteen, which was when she really got to know him for the first time. She is now very close to her dad, acting as one of his primary caretakers during medical emergencies and making sure he has what he needs week to week.

The experience of observing the dynamic between her separated parents, and also between Cornbread and his estranged son, caused Jennifer to think twice about pursuing music professionally. "Growing up with my father, seeing my brother leave the family for music, and then watching my father and all of his relationships that he's had, it kind of gave me a sour taste in my mouth with music. And I didn't want to grow up to be like that," she reflected. She still loved to sing but was happy keeping it to a hobby. "I love music so much. And I never wanted to lose that, and I never wanted to put anything before the people I love. But music is very powerful. It's beautiful. And it's everything. I grew up in the bars, at Nikki's Cafe downtown watching my dad play, you know, and it was just out of this world."

IN 1985, around the time when his marriage to Carol ended and he was forced to watch another child drift out of his life, Cornbread experienced something of a creative rebirth while playing with the Ice Blue Blues Band, also known simply as ICE. By this time he had settled in North Minneapolis and purchased the home where he still lived when we met. It was there that he connected with a musician in the neighborhood named Joe Rowe who would become a close friend and significant creative collaborator.

Whereas Cornbread had spent the bulk of his career performing in what one might describe, in large brushstrokes, as white venues for audiences of predominantly white diners, drinkers, and dancers—from the teen dance halls of his Augie Garcia days to the supper clubs on Lake Minnetonka and swanky piano bars of downtown Minneapolis—Rowe's experiences more closely mirrored those of other Black artists from the North Side who were struggling to make a living playing traditionally Black music like the blues.

This was an era when Prince was at the height of his fame with *Purple Rain*; Jimmy Jam and Terry Lewis were scoring major hits writing and producing artists like the S.O.S. Band, Cherrelle, and Alexander O'Neal; and dozens of wannabe superstars and eagle-eyed A&R execs were streaming into the Twin Cities in search of the newfangled Minneapolis Sound that combined traditionally Black art forms like R&B, soul, and the blues with electronic dance beats, new wave synthesizers, and modern rock guitar playing.

Even as a new generation of Black artists were putting Minneapolis on the map, musicians of Cornbread's generation like Joe Rowe noticed a troubling trend: the scene's Black predecessors and cultural practitioners were being edged out.

With the Ice Blue Blues Band, Rowe, who performed as JaJa Lateef, sought to "bring the *real* blues, Black blues, back to the Twin Cities." Speaking to the North Minneapolis newspaper *Insight News* in May 1985, Rowe said, "You got to be Black to have lived through the suffering. . . . To have a feeling, like you'd get from listening to your grandparents. Look at the great players, B. B. King, Albert King, and a whole bunch more. They knew that feeling."

The reporter for the paper, Arnold Stead, agreed with Rowe's assessment that the blues was nearing a point of extinction in the local scene. "That the field of Black bluesmen, resident in the Twin Cities, is near zero cannot be denied," he wrote. "The blues clubs here import their Black performers from Chicago, even then these clubs have a tough go of it. Artists that fill stadiums in Germany and Japan are lucky to fill a saloon in Minnesota."

With the Ice Blue Blues Band, Rowe and Cornbread worked up a robust repertoire of standards that included the blues as well as some jazz and R&B songs. Cornbread, the eldest of the group,

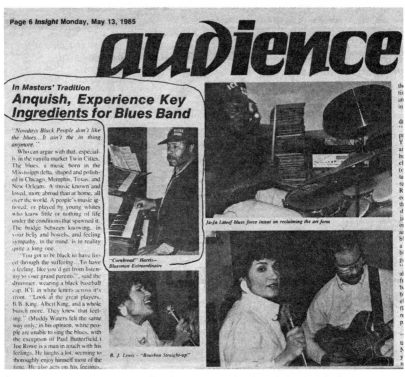

An *Insight News* clipping from Cornbread's scrapbook includes handwritten annotations from the artist. The article on the ICE blues band was published on May 13, 1985. Courtesy of Cornbread Harris.

played keyboards and sang, Rowe played drums, and Lewis James joined in on guitar. A woman named B. J. Lewis entered the mix when she asked Cornbread if he knew how to get ahold of his chart-topping son. According to the *Insight* article, "The veteran keyboardist didn't know the whereabouts of his offspring," but once he and his bandmates heard Lewis sing, they invited her to join the group. Later on, the lineup would evolve into a trio with Jim Levy on guitar.

Looking back on his days in the Ice Blue Blues Band, Cornbread said he appreciated the fact that it was a true collaboration with his friend Joe Rowe. "We were co-leaders of the band. And that kinda reminds me of Jimmy and Terry, you know, two guys working together—and actually working together, not fighting each other or nothing," he noted. "Agreeing and getting something done together. Ice Blues band went quite well."

After spending nearly a year woodshedding in Joe Rowe's dining room and recording a demo tape of some of their favorite standards (including "Saturday Nite Fish Fry," "In the Dark," and "C. C. Rider"), the band started playing out and quickly earned the respect of their peers. By the end of the '80s they would perform at the Riverview Supper Club, a Minnesota Black Musicians Awards ceremony at Orchestra Hall, and the massive RiverFest on Harriet Island in St. Paul. In a preview of the 1990 RiverFest event, the *Star Tribune* reported, "This Twin Cities band seems to surface only at RiverFest to play smokin', horn-accentuated blues."

BY THE END OF THE '80S, Cornbread's music career started gaining momentum in a way he hadn't experienced in decades. He credited this spike in activity and attention to the fact that he had finally reached the point where he could retire from his multiple day jobs, which toward the end included working for both the foundry and what he referred to as "the packing house," a slaughterhouse in South St. Paul where he wore out his arms stretching leather hides. Finally free of other commitments, he started saying yes to every single live performance opportunity that came his way.

Ask anyone who was active in the Twin Cities music scene in the 1990s when they learned about Cornbread Harris, and they will likely say that they first saw him either down at Nikki's Cafe in the Warehouse District, or at the old Loring Bar on Loring Park. Cornbread estimates that between those two venues he must have played hundreds, if not thousands, of shows in that decade; in the process, he solidified his reputation as a heartfelt, charming, endlessly entertaining live performer who was as much

Cornbread plays the piano in the basement bar of Nikki's Cafe, where he had a long residency in the 1990s and recorded his first live album. Photograph by Jimmy Steinfeldt.

a part of the atmosphere at these establishments as the food and drinks.

It was Cornbread's weekly residency at Nikki's Cafe that earned him his first piece of major local press. On November 1, 1990, the *Star Tribune* ran a profile of Cornbread written by the veteran music critic Jon Bream. More than forty years into his career, it was the first time that his life's work and his story had received such a glowing spotlight.

"Harris knows his way around a piano," Bream wrote. "During a solo he may take listeners on a tour of America's favorite blues towns—Kansas City, Chicago, and New Orleans. His instrumental excursions invariably define the mood of a piece. He leans toward a happy, almost club-style blues." The article noted that Cornbread had worked up more than a hundred songs to include in his repertoire, with a special focus on the blues, in addition to nearly fifty songs that he'd composed himself. It also highlighted how he loved to take requests. "I'm a public servant," Cornbread told the paper. "I'll play for the king, I'll play for the queen. I'll play for the bums on the street. I'm there to play."

When I read this article to Cornbread, he squealed with delight and clapped his hands in approval. "Oh, they got me down to a T! They really nailed it," he said, beaming. "Nikki's was kind of my start-out place on my fame trip. I held jam sessions. And the musicians would come in to play with me. And I would have them come and do whatever they could do. Yeah, blow your horn, play your drums, play your bongos, shake your tambourine. You know, whatever. Come on in and we'll play music together. And it worked out really beautiful."

The first musician to join Cornbread at Nikki's was his nephew, Renee Phiefer, whom Cornbread taught to play the drum kit shortly before he started up the Nikki's residency. "I always played the drums but never *played* the drums until I got with my uncle, who helped me learn how to play," Phiefer told me. "I played the drums with him from 1990 to '92. So I played a few years."

When asked about what it was like to be in a band with Corn-bread, Renee said, "Well, I was with my uncle, so it was fun. I en-joyed myself. I mean, people came from all over to see us. I met a lot of people from all over the world."

Because of the proximity of Nikki's to other musical hot spots like the Fine Line, the New French Café, Metro Studio, and several rehearsal warehouses, Renee said that there were often music industry bigwigs passing through and taking interest in their performances. "I mean, there was a lot of times that record companies would come up to us and say how much they loved us. And they'd say they'd call us and then wouldn't call, and that was the way it was. And sometimes when we were at Nikki's, Prince's band would be playing across the street. They would come over when they were taking a break to listen to Cornbread and me play music."

"I remember seeing him out there a lot," said Tommy Bar-barella, a founding member of Prince's New Power Generation who also played occasionally at Nikki's. "I hung out there a lot. I loved [proprietor] Nikki [Reisman]. She would always be at the bar. And Cornbread had that harmonica holder around his neck, but it was a coat hanger? It was awesome."

Veteran local troubadour Paul Metsa also remembered first connecting with Cornbread at Nikki's. "He's one of our hidden heroes," Paul said. "I've always loved the guy—you can't help but love him. With Cornbread, it was as fun hanging out yakking on the break as it was to see him play. Guys like Cornbread and me, those house gigs were our bread and butter."

Metsa said that all these years later, he can still remember spe-cific songs that Cornbread played at Nikki's. "He played us this song, I think it was called 'Ghost Ship,' and it just knocked me out," he recalled. "It was like a '40s tune, a bluesy tune about this ghost ship—it just knocked me out. But that was the beauty of Cornbread: his repertoire was so vast. There were always nuggets that you'd stumble into. He's a storyteller's storyteller."

Cornbread was photographed in the Warehouse District of downtown Minneapolis, just outside Nikki's Cafe, in 1995, as part of a series of photographs created to promote his first CD, *Live at Nikki's.* Photograph by Jimmy Steinfeldt.

The drummer Jack Chaffee, who took over on the kit once Renee stopped gigging, said that performing alongside Cornbread at Nikki's taught him an important lesson about taking the job seriously. "Weeknights, I mean, sometimes we had three, four audience members. But Cornbread never cared how many people were in the audience, whether it was one person, or one hundred people. He was going to play his show from this time to that time, and we never stopped early. Doesn't matter who's there; if nobody's there, we're still playing. And that was just who he was. I always respected that."

Ever the hard-working hustler looking out for the next performance opportunity, Cornbread was able to parlay the buzz around his residency into all sorts of gigs throughout the rest of the '90s, from the Loring to regular stints playing on the riverboats that launched off Harriet Island in St. Paul. He has especially fond memories of holding down recurring gigs on the *Anson Northrup* riverboat, where he played countless special events.

"That's where I got into marriages and stuff, playing on the boat," Cornbread recalled. "People would hire the boat, they would get the music, and I would be the band. So that worked out quite good." By the mid-'90s, his schedule was packed with private parties, weddings, funerals, fundraisers, and galas that were booked by people who had seen him play on the boat or at one of his house gigs.

In 1995, Cornbread reached another career milestone: he recorded his first album of his own material, *Live at Nikki's*. Cornbread's longtime bass player and friend Scott Soule remembers the album well—he had just joined the band a month prior to the recording. "That was recorded on March 4 and 5, 1995," Scott recalled. He said that drummer Jack Chaffee had a big hand in making the record happen, and that other musicians were eager to come down and sit in. "Paul Sanders was one, Tom Zozel was

Cornbread *(left)* performed on the *Anson Northrup* riverboat in the mid-1990s and is photographed with the ship's captain. *Anson Northrup* is one of the historic paddleboats that launches from Harriet Island in St. Paul and takes guests on a cruise down the Mississippi River. Courtesy of Cornbread Harris.

Cornbread celebrates the creation of his first CD, *Live at Nikki's,* with his longtime bass player and friend Scott Soule at Noiseland Industries in 1996. Courtesy of Cornbread Harris.

on it, Clark Upton played the trumpet, and then Howard Wright was the guitar player. Brilliant man. The thing about Nikki's was it was a really nice sounding room, with wood floors. It was a good atmosphere. So that's why I think it became so popular for him."

Live at Nikki's begins with the sound of warm audience chatter and Cornbread's voice cutting through the din, telling the story of how he got his name and breaking into "The Cornbread Song." The interaction between the singer and his audience is immediately apparent; after each line you can hear people in the room whooping and egging him on, and by the time the whole band joins in you can practically feel the tables full of patrons bobbing their heads to the beat.

"He sort of had a regular crowd of people that would come see him—we had the Nikki's crowd," Jack Chaffee recalled. "And Cornbread would remember everybody. Oftentimes when he saw someone come in, he would play a song that he knew they liked.

It was common for a singer to come in, and he would see them and say, 'Come up and sing that song.' He would create an atmosphere in the room where everybody felt like they were a part of everything. Which was always really cool."

"Yeah, we had a lot of people who would come in there. There was a guy who lived around the corner who would come in practically every night," added Scott. "I mean, there were a lot of people who had relationships that were sort of solidified around the music of James Samuel 'Cornbread' Harris Sr."

Live at Nikki's was released on cassette tape in 1995 and on CD in the summer of 1996, and it earned Cornbread another round of positive local press, including at least one rave review. Finally, after nearly fifty years of performing regularly in the Twin Cities, he had been fully embraced by the area's tastemakers and scenesters as an important figure in local music—a legacy that would continue to be solidified over the next thirty years of his ever-evolving career.

I LEARNED EARLY in my meetings with Cornbread that if he didn't recall something one week, I should ask him about it again the next. Sometimes it felt like heading out on a walk through the woods and hoping to see some wildlife along the way; with enough patience and persistence, something truly surprising might hop right in front of you on the path.

One day, while we were in the midst of getting set up to do a Zoom call with Jimmy, Cornbread and I started chatting about all the different times Prince and Jimmy had worked together, including their reunion in the film *Graffiti Bridge*. Not thinking anything of it, I asked Cornbread if he remembered any of the hubbub that might have happened locally while Prince was filming the movie out at his recording complex, Paisley Park, in Chanhassen.

"I got called by the people," he remembered. "They said, 'Is this Jimmy's dad?' I said, 'Yeah.' 'Oh, do you want to be in the movie?'"

I stopped fiddling with my recording equipment and looked up. "Wait, really?"

"Yeah! I said, 'Well, yeah, I want to be in the movie.' They said, 'Okay, come down to the curtain call,' or whatever they have. And so I was there with a bunch of people. Not no special guy or nothing. Just me and a whole bunch of people. And I did get into a walking scene, and a scene drunk in the alley or something. But I was in there. So, yeah, I'm pretty familiar with *Graffiti Bridge*."

"Well, that's a new one," I said, somewhat stunned by the revelation. "We haven't covered that yet. I'm going to have to watch that again."

"Yep," he said. "My biggest scene was when I was walking down the street with a bunch of people and some lady that was supposed to be my girlfriend or something. That was about my big scene."

Ostensibly a sequel to *Purple Rain*, Prince filmed *Graffiti Bridge* with the original members of The Time at Paisley Park in the winter of late 1989 and early 1990, around the time Cornbread was starting up his residency at Nikki's Cafe. Sure enough, when I went home and watched *Graffiti Bridge* that night, I caught a fleeting glimpse of Cornbread, decked out in a long white trench coat with a woman clutching his arm. The two of them walked through the background of a street scene in which The Time's Morris Day and Jerome Benton try to convince Prince's co-star Ingrid Chavez to get into their limousine, mixing in with a crowd of extras.

As we waited for Jimmy to join the Zoom, I told Cornbread we should ask him if he remembered his dad's role in the film. "I don't think I seen much of him in the whole movie thing, because he was a big star, he had a different room. We were extras out there, this big old bunch of people," Cornbread said. "But I got my little shot. It was like being on the field in a ballgame instead of in the stands, or watching it on TV. That was a whole different thing. And you know, I treasure it as a memory."

Once Jimmy logged on, I let them chat for a little bit before bringing up our latest discovery. "Jimmy, something we were just talking about, that Cornbread had not talked about with me before, is that he remembers that he had a part as an extra in *Graffiti Bridge*," I told him.

"I can't remember that," Jimmy said, seeming like he was caught off guard. "Do I remember that? I don't know whether I remember that."

"Well, we didn't get to see much of each other," Cornbread reminded him. "I was an extra."

"Do you remember what they were filming that day? Were you just there one day, or were you there more days?" Jimmy asked.

"I was there most of the time," Cornbread said. "But we'd have to sit and wait and wait, and then they'd pick out who they wanted for that scene. So I got picked a couple times. I remember one of my scenes was walking down the street with my girlfriend. And another was in the alley, just sitting there."

"I'm going to have to find that clip," Jimmy replied, then abruptly changed the subject. "Andrea, do you have another question?"

When I first learned that Cornbread had been involved in the film, I found it delightful and poignant, another in a long line of examples of how Cornbread contributed behind the scenes to the Minneapolis Sound of Prince and his peers. The more we talked about it, however, the more I understood that Cornbread's big movie set moment wasn't entirely positive. It happened at a point when he desperately wanted to reconnect with Jimmy, and being in such close proximity to his son but receiving something of a cold shoulder from him—while Cornbread played a bum in an alleyway and Jimmy was treated like movie-star royalty, no less— only served to add insult to injury and accentuate their discord.

When I mentioned *Graffiti Bridge* to Scott Soule, he noted, "Yeah, we have a song dedicated to that: 'Street People's Blues.'" Sure enough, when I went back through the recordings I'd gathered, I found a track on *Cornbread Supreme, Volume II* titled "Street People":

I've got a home in the alley
Yes, I roam the streets
Dig in trash cans for my food
Threw out some sweets

My friend, I see you
Rolling 'round in your big limousine
When you give me a handout
You're laughing at me it seems

Yes I've got children
Me they do not claim
All the good in their life, they did
For me, I gotta take the blame

I reach out for arms now
Love seems to be in the past
Gettin' a little old now
I don't know how much longer I'm gonna last

Put some money in my jar
So I can feed myself
If there's any left
I'm gonna share it with somebody else

Oh we're the street people
Yes we've paid our dues
Street people
And these are the street people's blues

On a separate day, a few weeks after our chat with Jimmy, Cornbread and I listened to the song together. "I played it at *Graffiti Bridge,* in that room," Cornbread said, remembering back to the film production at Paisley Park. He said he spent long hours waiting with the other extras to be called on the set, and he would pass the time by serenading the group on the piano. "That's the first time I believe I played it," he recalled. "Things were going through my mind at the time, and there it was—boom. 'Street People's Blues.'"

I asked Cornbread if he remembered Jimmy avoiding him on set, and he nodded. "Cold shoulder, yes. The little time he did spend there was, 'Oh, I gotta go.' So, yeah, that was a kind of loneliness; you're here, but you're not here."

Around the time that Cornbread and I started discussing the movie, I happened to have an interview for a separate project scheduled with the Minneapolis filmmaker Craig Rice, who worked with Prince on *Purple Rain* and *Graffiti Bridge*. On a whim, I thought I'd ask Craig if he remembered Cornbread being present on the set at Paisley Park.

"Yeah, I know Cornbread. I brought him to the movie," Craig replied, much to my surprise. "I was always trying to get Jimmy to get back to his dad. I mean, 'Yes, I know he did wrong. I'm not trying to make up for the past. But it's your *dad*, Jimmy.' So when we were making the movie, I could do what I wanted to do, because I produced the movie, so I brought his dad out to be on the set so he could see. They didn't connect; I know Jimmy was not wildly pleased that I brought him out."

"Cornbread—when I was a musician, he was the elder for us as musicians," Craig continued. "He and Baby Doo [Catson] and Lazy Bill Lucas, those are the cats you gotta respect, because they were the ones that were here when the rest of us were dinking around trying to figure out what to play."

It was clear that Jimmy wasn't eager to reminisce more about this period, so I didn't press him any further about it. At some point I had surpassed the typical journalist–source relationship and had clearly developed a friendship with both him and Cornbread, which I felt no need to resist. Still, I found myself wondering about where the line was, between gathering enough facts about someone's life to write a biography about them and inserting oneself too far, getting too personal, asking for too much.

This especially nagged at me the further we got into retracing their separation. How much did I really need to know—especially when they both seemed to regard the most painful points of their relationship as ancient history? Was it actually helping either of them to force that pain back up to the surface? Or was that what they needed to fully heal?

CORNBREAD, JIMMY, AND I all share a few personality traits that you might describe as Minnesotan. We are all exceedingly cordial, careful about managing others' feelings, and skilled in the art of conflict avoidance. Given the abandonment that both men experienced in their youth—Cornbread with the tragic loss of both parents in his early childhood, and Jimmy with the departure of his dad during his pivotal teen years—they both became professional people-pleasers and had become equally adept at navigating every conversation back to a place of positivity and laughter.

It occurred to me, after we'd gotten a few months into our gatherings as a trio, that aside from their very first meeting at Cornbread's daycare center that summer, every interaction that Cornbread was able to have with Jimmy was orchestrated by me, theoretically for the purpose of contributing to this book, and took place with a tape recorder running. Our meetings were unfolding like acts in a grand performance, with me in the audience and two natural-born performers onstage.

That same winter, I was introduced to the philosopher and author Parker J. Palmer's concept of "third things," which he writes about in his book *A Hidden Wholeness*:

> In Western culture, we often seek truth through confrontation. But our headstrong ways of charging at truth scare the shy soul away. If soul truth is to be spoken and heard, it must be approached "on the slant." I do not mean we should be coy, speaking evasively about subjects that make us uncomfortable, which weakens us and our relationships. But soul truth is so powerful that we must allow ourselves to approach it, and it to approach us, indirectly. We must invite, not command, the soul to speak. We must allow, not force, ourselves to listen.
>
> We achieve intentionality in a circle of trust by focusing on an important topic. We achieve indirection by exploring that topic metaphorically, via a poem, a story, a piece of music, or a work of art that

embodies it. I call these embodiments "third things" because they represent neither the voice of the facilitator nor the voice of a partici- pant. They have voices of their own, voices that tell the truth about a topic but, in the manner of metaphors, tell it on the slant. Mediated by a third thing, truth can emerge from, and return to, our awareness at whatever pace and depth we are able to handle—sometimes inwardly in silence, sometimes aloud in community—giving the shy soul the protective cover it needs.

Along the way, I recognized that this book project became Corn- bread's, Jimmy's, and my "third thing." It gave us a reason to gather and offered us something to work on together that wasn't necessarily about their reconciliation, but it opened the long- closed doors in both of them to talk about it nonetheless. Like good Minnesotans and tenderhearted artistic people, we were approaching it "on the slant."

The time that Cornbread and Jimmy got to spend together felt incredibly precious, and our conversation about *Graffiti Bridge* was a good reminder to proceed gently around these thornier mo- ments from their past, lest I risk souring whatever remaining time they had to be together. What mattered most to Cornbread in this late stage of his life was whatever was happening *right now*, and so as our calls carried on and became a routine, the three of us found a way to balance my need to gather information with their desire to just enjoy one another's company. Letting go of any ex- pectations I might have had at the outset of our collaboration, we settled into a joyful, peaceful rhythm that allowed the next stage of their relationship to slowly, beautifully unfold.

Chapter 7

ALL THE FUN

Well now please remember
When all is said and done
Don't forget to tell your friends
You had all the fun
—"All the Fun," Cadillac Kolstad and Cornbread Harris

Ever the restless creative mind, once Cornbread figured out how the Zoom technology worked, he started trying to find ways to bend it to his will. And even though Jimmy was half a country away from him, he was determined to find a way for the two of them to make music together again.

One afternoon, as soon as Jimmy's face popped up onto the screen, Cornbread launched into his idea. "Hey!" he said, skipping over their usual small talk. "Okay, so when I come out to wherever you are, and I'm going to come up onstage, this is what you've got to play, okay?"

Jimmy smiled and nodded his head. "Okay."

Cornbread swiveled around on his piano bench while I picked up the iPad and focused the camera on his hands as he played the opening refrain of his theme song "Blue Blue Blue Blues."

"That's it," Cornbread said. "That'll be my theme song, for all my life."

"That's like B. B. King," Jimmy commented, humming King's trademark opening guitar lick.

"Oh man, I wanted to play with that dude so bad," Cornbread said. "So I guess I will when I get to heaven. I'm going to have God hook us up."

"That'll be a good jam session," Jimmy responded. "But you know, you keep the spirit of what he does alive, you know?"

"Oh, well thank you, kind sir," Cornbread said, bowing his head.

"By the way," Jimmy asked, "how did you get the name Cornbread?"

"I wrote a song called Cornbread!" his dad responded proudly, turning toward his keys again and plunking out the opening chords. "Cornbread in the morning," he sang, "cornbread at night. Cornbread in the forenoon—everything will be all right."

As Cornbread played, another sound appeared in the background: it was Jimmy, tentatively poking out a few notes to see if he could get into the same key as his dad.

Cornbread stopped and looked over his shoulder.

"Can you hear this?" Jimmy asked, throwing out a smoking hot blues lick.

"Whoo! I think so," Cornbread said and then eagerly responded with a lick of his own.

"I need to adjust mine to yours. You need a piano tuning," Jimmy said, fiddling with his keyboard to adjust the modulation. Cornbread squealed with delight. "Well, I think it comes across in the same key," he replied, rubbing his hands together and waiting for more.

After a moment of silence, a sound rang out across the Zoom call: Jimmy was playing the opening riff of "The Cornbread Song."

"Yeah, that's the same thing!" Cornbread said. "Okay, play a phrase and stop. And then I'll see if I can copy the phrase," he instructed.

"I know you can," Jimmy said.

And just like that, Jimmy and Cornbread started talking— really talking—to each other, using the musical language that they both knew so well. It started with riffs on "The Cornbread Song," one playing and then the other shooting an idea back, then building on the phrase and developing it into something new. With the way both of their faces lit up, you could tell that they were communicating something through the music that was more meaningful than anything they'd said out loud to each other those past few months.

Halfway through, Jimmy stopped to adjust his keyboard again. "I put a Wurlitzer sound on, because I remembered you had that Wurlitzer," he explained. "But let me see if I can switch it into piano now."

They continued on, one piano lick after another, Cornbread dutifully copying every lick that Jimmy played, and Jimmy throwing back another interpretation.

"Okay, I go boomp and then you go boomp," Cornbread instructed, and pretty soon they were both comping and soloing, connectivity lags be damned.

"Yeah, yeah, yeah!" Cornbread said, swiveling back around to face the screen. "Call-and-response. I just got to play with Jimmy Jam!"

Without missing a beat, Jimmy replied, "I got to play with Cornbread!"

"Oh, man, that was really good," Cornbread said, shaking his head. "What a wonderful evening this is turning out to be."

Before we got off the call, Cornbread threw out the gentlest of pitches to his son. "If we ever get a show booked here with me and you, at the Hook and Ladder, you know, that'll be like a $25, $30 ticket. And if it's announced today, the tickets'll be all sold tomorrow. And it'll be like—I know it's cheap for you—it'll be like $900 a man, that you get paid. I know I can't play cheap with you," he said.

Although I'd heard Cornbread talk many times about his dream of playing onstage with Jimmy again, this was the first time he shared his dream with his son directly. Jimmy didn't really commit one way or another in the moment but seemed to smile at the idea and take it seriously.

"About the only truth I got in my life is how blessed I am," Cornbread continued, sighing and relaxing now that he had gotten his proposal out of the way. "From the day that I was sitting in the daycare center, and the lady comes over to me and says, 'You have a visitor.' I was just so happy to see you. Oh, man, that was so beautiful. And I never knew it would turn into something as great as what's happening here," he said, gesturing between himself and Jimmy on the screen. "Like I say, I really would like to get that show together at the Hook and Ladder. Sell it out! That's only one of a hundred shows for you. But it'll be one of the great ones."

Finally, after so much buildup and anticipation and wondering, an invitation had gone out over the Internet from Cornbread to Jimmy, extended like an outstretched hand. In the coming weeks, as we continued our regular calls, we would eagerly await his RSVP.

AS I WAS PACKING UP to leave that day, I decided to linger for a while in the hallway that leads from Cornbread's dining room up to his bedroom and front door so I could study all the accolades and photographs that lined every inch of the walls. I realized that the framed awards and plaques that hung there told a story about not just his performing career but his role in the community, particularly in North Minneapolis. In the 1990s especially, Cornbread was celebrated by several major community leaders and institutions; not only was this a decade when retirement allowed him to throw himself into filling his gig calendar, but it was also a time when he fully embraced his gift for mentoring others and began taking on a more official role as a music teacher and guiding light for the next generation of aspiring local artists.

Among the awards was an official proclamation signed by former Minneapolis Mayor R. T. Rybak that declared October 27,

A portrait of Cornbread was taken for the *Star Tribune* by staff photographer Carlos Gonzalez, who has documented Cornbread's career closely in the later decades of his life. Photograph by Carlos Gonzalez. Copyright 2006 Star Tribune.

2004, "The Twin Cities Music Legends' Day," celebrating the fact that numerous legends in the Minnesota music scene had been making music for over a century. Cornbread was listed on the proclamation alongside Percy Hughes, Doris Hines, Dick Mayes, Irv Williams, and others. Before putting the proclamation into a frame, he had circled his name in pen along with the words "over a century," where he added an asterisk and wrote "almost."

Down the wall a bit farther hung a certificate of commendation signed by former Minnesota Governor Arne Carlson, which recognized Cornbread's role as a teacher with the Citysongs program hosted by the University of Minnesota's School of Social Work and the Hallie Q. Brown Center. He also had plaques recognizing his role guiding youth at the Metropolitan Cultural Arts Inner City Theatre in the early '90s, and for teaching students at the Capri Theater in the same period as part of their 4H program, alongside numerous awards from the Greater Twin Cities Blues Music Society, the Minnesota Association of Songwriters, the Minnesota Black Music Awards, and the Rock Country Hall of Fame. And that didn't even include all the memorabilia that was crammed on top of his piano in his dining room.

"I got a lot of little plastic cups," he said, showing off the various accolades he'd collected. "This is the blues honor award, this is the jazz honor award. It's an amazing thing, I got more awards and pictures on the wall: there ain't room for 'em no more, hardly," he added, shaking his head. "Man."

At the end of the hallway, in the space just outside his bedroom door and alongside these other achievements, were two photographs of Cornbread with musicians whom he'd proudly mentored and helped shape: his son, Jimmy, and his longtime collaborator Cadillac Kolstad, who helped him to usher in yet another era of creative rebirth and resurgence in the mid-2000s.

Looking back over the eighty years that Cornbread has been a consistent presence in the Twin Cities music scene, it's remarkable to note that he experienced moments that you might describe as comebacks or resurgences at least once each decade.

Always hustling for the next gig, Cornbread has a long history of printing his own DIY business cards to carry with him at shows. The peace sign became a recurring logo for him over the years. Courtesy of Cornbread Harris.

That's the thing about enduring and sticking with one's craft in an industry that is liable to churn through new talent and burn people out: the longer Cornbread kept playing, the more opportunities he had to introduce himself to entirely new generations of fans.

STARTING IN THE LATE '90S, Cornbread began appearing in numerous theater productions in addition to playing his recurring house gigs. One of his first big forays into theater took place in the restaurant Gianni Fragali Italia Cucina, which was located in the Lumber Exchange Building in downtown Minneapolis. Billed as an interactive dinner show set in a 1920s New York speakeasy, the play *Gianni Sent Me* initially earned mixed reviews. ("You might go for the food, or the boogie-woogie music of bluesman Cornbread Harris, but don't expect good theater," *Star Tribune* critic Rohan Preston wrote.) But it found a loyal audience and ran for several years, keeping Cornbread booked well into 2001.

After dipping his toes into the theater world, he also performed in several other stage productions, including the well-received *Interview with Paul Robeson* that brought him on a regional tour of new venues that included the Varsity Theater in Minneapolis, the Off-Broadway Theatre in Milwaukee, and a long run at the Mabel Tainter Center for the Arts in Menomonie, Wisconsin. "This one went over really big," Cornbread said. The actor and vocalist Paul Mabon starred as Paul Robeson, the influential performer who was targeted during the McCarthy era for his support of the civil rights movement, while Cornbread held the role of Robeson's longtime accompanist, Lawrence Brown.

As Cornbread's performance opportunities continued to expand at the dawn of the new millennium, the two venues where he made a name for himself as a solo entertainer in the '90s both shuttered within a few months of one another. He performed at a farewell block party for the Loring Cafe and Bar at the end of May 2002, when it closed its location on Loring Park and began transitioning all of its regular musicians to a new location on a high-traffic corner in the heart of Dinkytown. The next month, he returned to Nikki's Cafe to play one last gig before the restaurant closed its doors for good.

The Loring Pasta Bar opened in 2001, and by 2003 Cornbread was one of the restaurant's regular acts, holding down a popular Friday night residency that stretched on for much of the early 2000s. Located at the epicenter of the University of Minnesota bar district, the Loring Pasta Bar residency introduced Cornbread not just to fine diners but to an entire generation of college students hitting up the restaurant's happy hours.

It was at the pasta bar where Cornbread would cross paths with one of his most significant collaborators of the new century, Andrew "Cadillac" Kolstad. In the summer of 2006, Cadillac started holding down a late-night slot on Friday nights immediately following Cornbread's dinnertime show. Ever the curious musician, Cornbread started hanging around after his time slot to check out the talented young pianist, who seemed to channel the same music and ethos from a bygone era that he did.

Eventually he started sitting in with Cadillac, hovering over the top of the piano and soloing while Cadillac pounded out bass notes and chords on the low end. By the following year, they were playing gigs together billed as "Cadillac vs. Cornbread," playing up a friendly rivalry that was actually more of a budding mentor–mentee relationship.

"Right now I follow Cornbread around. I watch everything he does, I listen to everything he does, I try to copy everything he does," Cadillac told *City Pages* in 2009. Journalist Max Ross described their unique chemistry onstage together: "When both pianists are present . . . watching them play is like being transported to a different age. The legend and his already-accomplished apprentice trade barbs and acoustic riffs without the aid of synthesizers or Vocoders. It's a return to something simpler than most modern music, but also something that's more lasting."

Cadillac liked to describe his music as "Mississippi River

A printed flyer for Cornbread's residency with Cadillac Kolstad advertises "A knock down, drag out make your woman shout bout" at Palmer's Bar every Sunday night. A line from Cornbread's song "Deeper Blues" appears at the top of the flyer. Courtesy of Cornbread Harris.

music," a nod to the Dixieland jazz and New Orleans blues that paddled upstream to Minneapolis over the previous century, picking up other regional styles of midcentury music along the way. A history buff who dressed like Jerry Lee Lewis (complete with a slicked-back pompadour), Cadillac booked all his gigs on a rotary dial telephone and drove to them in a 1964 Cadillac. The young artist seemed uniquely situated to latch on to Cornbread's style of piano playing and singing and promote it without attempting to modernize it for a new era.

"Traditionally, the role of the musician is one who communes with the ancestors, throughout all time," Cadillac told the author Cyn Collins in 2006 for her book *West Bank Boogie.* "The musician's role has always been helping people understand the context of what you're doing here now, where you came from and where you're going." Given Cadillac's passion for preserving cultural history, it only made sense that he and Cornbread eventually

143

settled into the longtime West Bank staple Palmer's Bar for their dueling Cadillac vs. Cornbread piano nights. Cadillac's father, "Papa" John Kolstad, started his career on the West Bank in the '60s and early '70s and raised his son surrounded by the folk and blues legends from that era. And there was something extra poetic about having Cornbread, who in the early 2000s was already well into his eighth decade, perform inside a historic time capsule of a dive bar that opened shortly before he was born.

Reflecting on those Cadillac vs. Cornbread shows years later, Cornbread still harbored the same competitive spirit that defined their collaboration. "There was no contest between me playing and him playing," Cornbread told me one day, a glint in his eye. "I'll wipe that dude out."

THE MUSICIANS' RESIDENCY was captured for posterity on the 2010 live album *All the Fun*. Over eight tracks, the camaraderie and playfulness of these gigs are audible; songs are accompanied by the constant hum of bar chatter and whoops from the crowd, and at times it's hard to tell whether Cadillac or Cornbread are working the low end of the piano with their boogie-woogie beats. They take turns singing lead, with Cornbread offering spirited renditions of "Mary Lou," "Cool Rider," "Deeper Blues," and "The Cornbread Song," and Cadillac name-checking his mentor (and razzing him) with the songs "Cornbread, Cornbread (Stole My Gal)" and the title track "All the Fun," which is something of a love letter to the experience of seeing them play together at Palmer's:

> The phone rang in the morning
> Down at Palmer's Bar
> Mike answered the telephone
> Open? Sorry, yes we are
> Can't give out no numbers
> I could call around
> With a little investigation

I'm sure your daughter will be found
The voice said, We're looking for our daughter
We'd really love to have her back
Last time she was seen leaving out the door with Mr. Cadillac
She had been missing for twelve hours or more
Last time she was seen with Cadillac and Cornbread running out
    that door

As you go through life
And you live to tell this tale
You may get on in years
You may get old and frail
Well now remember
When the dirty deed is done
Don't forget to tell your friends
You had all the fun

Come on down to Palmer's
The place that I know best
I tell you the truth, I guarantee
It's the gateway to the Wild, Wild West
Come on down to Palmer's
When you have nothing left to give
The best part about Palmer's, it only looks expensive

Come onto the bar
Get yourself a shot
When you stay all night you'll have to give it everything you've got
It's okay if you don't remember all you've said and done
Don't forget to tell your friends where you had all the fun

"The people there liked both of us," Cornbread recalled. "So they said, why don't you guys play together? So we did for quite a while. And that was a pretty good seller."

When I listened back to *All the Fun* with him in his dining room, Cornbread was eager to point out the saxophone playing of his longtime collaborator Jimmy "Jimmyapolis" Wallace, who takes an especially soulful solo on the live recording of "Deeper Blues." Much like how he spoke about his early days playing with

Willy Brown, Cornbread loved to gush about the time he spent onstage with Jimmy Wallace and another local sax legend, Dean Brewington.

"Dean Brewington, oh man. Him and Jimmy Wallace used to do duets," he said, sighing. "Man, I had a horn section then! I mean, when we would blow and then they would come in with harmonic lines, the same rhythm with the different tones so that it would be parallel? It would sound like four horns because of the harmony. Man. And I'm just plunking, you know? That's why I'm a blessed dude, because I've just had so much good luck."

Scott Soule remembered that Jimmy Wallace first entered Cornbread's orbit back in 1997 when he was holding down a house gig at the short-lived bistro Backstage at Bravo, which sat next door to the Orpheum Theater in downtown Minneapolis. "We were going to the gig one night, and here comes Jimmy striding down the street," Scott said. "We invited him to come and play with us, and it just clicked. He was really good at doing these on-the-spot arrangements. So he joined our group and kind of became musical director in a way, and then we had Dean Brewington come in to play alto saxophone."

These were musicians who would stick with Cornbread for decades, well into his Cadillac vs. Cornbread days at Palmer's and continuing with the house gigs he held down after the pandemic in the 2020s.

ANOTHER MEMORY THAT RETURNED to Cornbread while listening to the live recordings of him playing with Cadillac was the trip that they made together to Memphis, Tennessee, for the International Blues Challenge in 2011. Cornbread had already gone to Memphis once to participate in the challenge as a solo artist in 2008, and after winning a contest hosted by the Greater Twin Cities Blues Music Society with Cadillac in 2010, the two of them headed back down to perform with their collaborative act.

"I went down there, and Cadillac went down there," Cornbread recalled. "He did pretty good. I kind of flunked out because I wasn't playing the washboard-tub-with-the-string-type blues. And that's what they wanted to hear. I mean, my blues, which is really great—that wasn't the kind of music they wanted to hear. Because people don't realize how many different ways you can play the blues. So I found that out. I didn't have any problems with the customers: I had problems with the judges. The judges, they were saying, 'No, that ain't no blues.' So I couldn't win that one."

It was fascinating hearing Cornbread reflect on his experience, given his decades of experience playing the blues and developing it into a style that's all his own. It was also fascinating discovering a printed program from the International Blues Challenge in a binder in Cornbread's basement, and noting that at eighty-two years old, Cornbread was one of the only elders and one of the few Black artists pictured among the dozens of blues bands that traveled to Memphis to compete.

"I got ruled out of that one. But I did go, and I did play," Cornbread said. "And it was at one of B. B. King's nightclubs! He was already gone, you know, but the nightclub was still there. I always wanted to play with him, but I got to play at his club. So that was a big thing."

On a freezing cold evening just after New Year's Day in January 2023, Cadillac returned to Minneapolis from his new home in Salzburg, Germany, to share a piano with Cornbread once again. Word got out on social media that Cadillac was in town, and Palmer's Bar filled to the brim with fans of both artists to cheer on their reunion.

"Who are all you people? Get out of my bar!" one of the Palmer's regulars yelled, not a hint of sarcasm or humor in his voice. After attending several of Cornbread's Sunday evening gigs at Palmer's, I'd never seen anything quite like it. The crowd's cheers between songs sounded more like a sports arena than the typical mellow applause and whoops that usually punctuated Cornbread's shows, and once Cadillac set up an old-timey microphone

Cornbread and Cadillac are reunited at Palmer's Bar in January 2023. Photograph by Cheryl Wilson. Courtesy of Cadillac Kolstad.

and started singing to the crowd, it felt like the whole bar might tilt to one side.

Seemingly unfazed by the hubbub, Cornbread kept his head down and plunked away at the piano keys, assuming the same hunched position that he would any other night. One of the many charming things about seeing Cornbread play at Palmer's is that he performed at the bar's beat-up old upright, which was kept on the floor in the front corner of the bar next to the pinball machine and dartboard rather than up on the venue's tiny stage. Cornbread's band, which could include anywhere from four to eight or more players depending on the night, simply crowded into the corner around him, his back turned to the band as they all played. On this particular night, it looked like the audience of onlookers might swallow the band whole, or at the very least knock over his pint glass filled with his "Cornbread Special" (a custom nonalcoholic cocktail made up of equal parts orange, pineapple, and grapefruit juice) with their tipsy dancing and swaying. Cornbread and the band just kept playing all the same.

Looking around the crowded bar that night, it occurred to

me that if not for the way people were dressed, it would be impossible to discern whether their Cadillac vs. Cornbread reunion was taking place in 2023, or 2007, or 1954, or 1928. The venue, still outfitted with its original pressed-tin ceiling tiles and old wooden bar, certainly hadn't changed much in the century-plus of its lifespan, and the musicians' boogie-woogie, jazz, and blues music could just as well have been made in any of the dozen or so preceding decades.

Cadillac was right when he said that music offered a unique way to commune with our ancestors and to connect with the culture of our recent past. What Cornbread offered to the room that night, and to bars full of patrons every time he played, was a living, breathing connection to our own history—a throughline that wove the past century of musical heritage into the present moment. That night, as we all looked on and hollered our appreciation, I couldn't help but think about how lucky we were that Cornbread was still with us, still shuffling his way out to Palmer's every Sunday, and still plugging away at his craft for a fickle music scene that has gone through an endless cycle of embracing him, taking him for granted, forgetting him, and rediscovering him yet again.

Chapter 8

PUT THE WORLD BACK TOGETHER

Haven't we had enough debate?
Did I hear someone say, "Let's wait"?
Why don't we get together before it's too late?
—"Put the World Back Together," Cornbread Harris

The first time I heard Cornbread play his song "Put the World Back Together" was the day we met in the studios of Minnesota Public Radio in 2017. Although we hadn't yet experienced the global pandemic and citywide racial unrest that would completely upend our lives, it was already a heavy time in America. We were just half a year into the Trump era, and a fight over the former president's so-called Muslim Ban had made it all the way to the Supreme Court, saturating the daily news cycle with conversations about who should and shouldn't be allowed to live among us.

That summer the toxic political climate felt like it could swallow us all whole. But then in walked Cornbread with his gentle demeanor and his nine decades of hard-earned wisdom, and as soon as he sat down to play it felt like the whole broken outside world dissolved away. In that moment in time, the only thing that remained was Cornbread and his beautiful music.

"I'm writing new songs all the time," Cornbread told us that day. As he gently moved his hands through the chord progressions, he sang clearly and somberly, almost venturing into spoken word as he enunciated each line.

> Haven't we had enough debate?
> Did I hear someone say, "Let's wait"?
> Why don't we get together before it's too late?
> Put the world back together
> Put the world back together
> Put the world back together again
>
> Ride in the country
> Sounds insane
> Smell your polluted water
> Feel your acid rain
> Cut down your forests, why don't you?
> Plant 'em back again
> Put the world back together
> Put the world back together
> Put the world back together again
>
> Politicians are talking fear and hate
> I heard someone say, "Let's have a war"
> Blow 'em all away (that's stupid!)
> Can't you hear me when I say?
> Put the world back together
> Put the world back together
> Put the world back together again

Each time he wound into the chorus, he waved to my co-host and me to indicate that we should sing along with him. Not wanting to ruin the crystal-clear recording of him performing his music alone at the piano, we hesitated and stayed quiet, but he kept motioning to us to join him all the same. In retrospect, it's probably one of the only times in his career he wasn't able to cajole onlookers into singing with him and uniting a room in call-and-response. Part of me regrets leaving him hanging, but I do treasure the recording that he made in the studio that day, because it captures his voice in all its vulnerability, wisdom, and optimism. It has clearly had an effect on others as well: at the time of writing this, the YouTube video of Cornbread singing "Put the World Back Together" in The Current's studio has been viewed more than twelve thousand times.

"Let's listen to our elders," one commenter wrote. "Ninety years of living gives simple clarity." Another added, "We are here for you, Cornbread Harris! Many thanks for your gentle love."

When he played the song for us that day, he told us he had just written it. And in the grand scheme of things, I suppose that is true; although it was released on his 2001 album *Cornbread Supreme, Volume 1,* he kept tweaking and rewriting the lines in the ensuing years of live performances. And besides, when considered in the vast timeline of his eighty-year career, a song he'd only written fifteen or twenty years ago *was* new, relatively speaking. The fact that lines that were likely inspired by post-9/11 warmongering sounded just as relevant in a completely different political era only accentuated how good Cornbread was at writing timeless, enduring songs.

After finishing the tune, he took a moment to reflect on the song's themes. "That would go along with my ministerial thing, to tell the people—look, you guys gotta look out for this world; you can't just keep polluting it and destroying it," he said. "You've gotta look out for your neighbors; you can't just be running over folks trying to get ahead of everybody. You know?"

Cornbread's "ministerial thing" had taken over a large part of his life by the time we met. In addition to his house gigs and his weekly trips to his daycare center, his annual Sunday morning outing to his neighborhood church, Zion Baptist, was a nonnegotiable part of his routine. He'd earned the honorary title of Deacon and spent every church service proudly seated in the front row and even had a special tambourine he brought with him each week so he could keep time with the choir while they performed.

When I spoke with Cornbread's daughter Jennifer about his faith, she told me that he became a deacon at the church—and

Cornbread performs in the studios of Minnesota Public Radio in the summer of 2017. Photograph from Minnesota Public Radio News and Minnesota Public Radio's The Current®. Copyright 2017 Minnesota Public Radio®. Reprinted with permission. All rights reserved.

became more devout and spiritual overall—following the tragic loss of his first daughter, Cynthia Harris, to cancer in late 2005 when she was fifty-five years old. It was a heartbreak that still weighed on Cornbread late in life.

"All I know is, she was my favorite person," he told me one day, remembering Cynthia. "She was just born with a good heart. She never was a bad child. She was always wanting to be helpful and loving and kind—and man, you cannot, unless you're evil, hate a person like that. There's very few people can stand up to that level of being a person, you know."

In the years following Cynthia's death, Cornbread seemed to be on a mission to model his own behavior after his late daughter's. He started attending Bible study classes, quit smoking, and generally mellowed out into the "blessed dude" and generous person I met when we first started working together.

"Yeah, he kind of lives by the rule," his longtime bass player and friend Scott Soule noted. "He's really into his church on Sundays and his Bible studies on Wednesdays, and he'll go on and on. The thing about it is, it's taught him to be thankful for everything, and everyone, every day. I think there's probably been times in his life when he wasn't like that. So it's a super positive influence on him; he's got a heart that's bigger than ten people, and I think that his faith has allowed him to get that."

CORNBREAD HAD TWO STORIES he liked to tell about God, and I heard them nearly every week we got together. Sometimes the stories were brief, and sometimes they would stretch on a little longer if he decided to embellish them with a few new details, but the essence of them pretty much stayed the same.

The first story had to do with his daily conversations with God. "I get high on saying thank you to God," he enthused. "He says to me, He says, 'How's it going, Cornbread?' I say, 'You know how it's goin'. It's goin' wonderful!' And He says, 'Are you sure that you really like that you've been blessed this much?' And I say, 'I'm sure that I really like it. I like it.' And He says, 'Well, hold on, buddy, because more is coming.' The more I say thank you to the Lord, God, Jehovah, Emmanuel, whatever—the more I say thank you to Him, the more He dumps on me."

His second story had to do with the angels that God sent down to Earth to dole out His blessings—the same angels that Cornbread was certain were responsible for grabbing the notes that he sang in midair and "polishing them up" before placing them in people's ears, causing everyone who heard them to fall in love with him.

"God got His angels together in heaven for a meeting," he liked to say, launching into the story. "And He's saying, 'Okay, I want such and such a family to be blessed,' and so forth. 'And I'm putting blessings in all you angels' bags. Putting blessings in these babies.' Just like Santa Claus, you know? So here come all these

Cornbread cues his band while performing at the Hook and Ladder. Photograph by Nate Ryan.

angels out, millions of angels coming out from heaven with bless-ings from God. And He pulled my angel aside and said, 'Look, don't sweat it about going all over with all this whole bunch of stuff. You go by Cornbread's house and just dump the whole bag of blessings on him.'"

The more he acknowledged his blessings and thanked God and everyone else, the more blessings rained down upon him. These were the explanations that he had come up with to make sense of the fact that all of the hardships of his past had now faded away and become distant memories, and that his life continued to evolve and open up in surprising and beautiful ways. How else to explain, he reasoned, how he had become such a blessed dude?

One day while calling to arrange a visit with Cornbread at his daycare facility, Augustana's Open Circle, the director Janine McQuillan took a few minutes to chat with me on the phone. "You know, Cornbread had us pray every week that Jimmy would come back to him," she said, her voice becoming emotional as she spoke. "Every single week, we would pray to God to bring Jimmy back into Cornbread's life. I couldn't believe it when I went to the front door one day and saw him. He was wearing dark sunglasses, a hat, and a mask, but I knew right away that it was him: that's Jimmy. He came back."

As I learned more about how that fateful day came to be, I couldn't help but note the similarities between the stories Cornbread told about God and His angels and the seemingly heaven-sent helpers that all unwittingly conspired to bring Jimmy back into Cornbread's life. Shortly before I began work on this book, a series of events unfolded that I would only learn about in detail much later, which involved a choir of Minneapolis punk rock and funk angels from every corner of the music scene.

IN JANUARY 2021, with the city still reeling from the murder of George Floyd and the coronavirus pandemic still raging, a freshly vaccinated Cornbread agreed to participate in a project hosted by the Hennepin County Public Library's MNSpin program that took place at the hip Loring Park hair salon and record shop HiFi Hair. Sitting down at the shop's well-worn, hand-painted piano, Cornbread played his song "Put the World Back Together" for passersby. The song immediately caught the attention of the store's owner, the omnipresent Minneapolis scenester and music booster Jon Clifford, who months later still remembered every detail of this moment vividly.

"Here was a ninety-three-year-old man playing his song 'Put the World Back Together' after the lockdown, George Floyd, and the riots. The unrest and the sadness. I just stood there and cried," Jon told me. He captured some of the performance on his phone and was so moved by the experience that he started telling anyone whom he crossed paths with about this incredible man and his poignant, timely song.

About a week later, Jon happened to be cutting the hair of Ricky Peterson, an accomplished keyboard player who has recorded and toured with countless musical legends, and whose late mother, Jeanne Arland Peterson, came up in the same time as Cornbread and was a musical icon in her own right. Jon played the video for Ricky and asked if he thought they could get Cornbread into a studio somewhere to record his beautiful song. "Absolutely, I'm in!" Ricky replied, easily convinced of the song's powers in the time it took to style his hair.

By the end of March, Ricky had rounded up his equally talented and esteemed brothers Billy and Paul Peterson and headed to Creation Audio with Jon, Cornbread, and the engineer Steve Weiss to lay down a short EP of Cornbread's songs, including "The Cornbread Song," "Blue Blue Blue Blues," and "Put the World Back Together." The resulting CD, *The Creation Session,* was for sale at HiFi Hair and other local record shops.

"Everybody was willing to do it out of their heart, you know, for Cornbread, because he was so cool, man, and we all knew who he was," Ricky Peterson said. "Our sister Patty had done a Minnesota jazz legends session with him a few years ago [for Jazz88 FM], and we all saw him perform there. That was done at Creation, too, and that's where I first met him—and unbeknownst to us, he was Jimmy's father."

As soon as the EP opens, you can hear Cornbread gasp and let out a laugh at how good it sounds to have all these polished musicians in a studio together, playing his songs in pristine recording quality. "The look of joy on Cornbread's face will be tattooed on my soul for my entire life," Jon said, while Paul Peterson remembered that they all "had a great time that day, just following him. It reminded me a lot of playing with mom in her later years. You know, let them do their thing and just enhance what they do, to bring them out. And Ricky did that beautifully."

Riding high on the energy from that recording session, Jon Clifford returned home and wrote a letter to Jimmy, explaining the project and asking if he might want to record a harmony for the chorus of "Put the World Back Together." Since Paul Peterson and Jimmy knew each other from the '80s music scene (Paul actually replaced Jimmy when he was fired by Prince from The Time and appeared in *Purple Rain* as the band's keyboardist), Jon asked Paul if he might be willing to send the note along, and a few days later, Paul sent it to Jimmy in a DM on Instagram.

"The Peterson brothers' motto is 'Make people say no,'" Paul explained later. "That means, in other words, just ask, right? Ask for whatever that it is you're looking for. And Jon wrote this beautiful letter about the project, about his father. And I just basically said in this Instagram direct message, 'Jimmy, I got no horse in this race. But I need you to know what we're doing with your father. We just did a record with my two brothers, and Jonny Clifford, he's written this letter to you, and I'm just going to send it to you and you do with it what you please.'"

Weeks went by, and no one heard anything. Then one day in May, without knowing that any of this had gone down, I reached out to Jimmy about a completely separate matter, asking him if he and Terry might like copies of the new paperback edition of my first book. He wrote back right away with the mailing address for their studio and then added: "Minneapolis was on my mind cause we're taking a quick trip there to film a piece for the Billboard Music Awards. . . . If you don't mind me asking, I was gonna try to see my dad while I was in town. I haven't been in touch with him. . . . I know he just did some stuff with Paul Peterson and he gave me a little info. But if there's anything you know, let me know."

My heart leapt. I reached out to Cornbread's longtime friend Chris Mozena, who runs the South Minneapolis venue the Hook and Ladder and who helped Cornbread with his business affairs, like promoting his gigs and pressing up live recordings of his shows. Chris immediately agreed to help facilitate a meeting between Cornbread and Jimmy, and after exchanging a few urgent texts, it seemed that the details would all fall into place. I tucked my phone away and wondered what might happen next.

A few days later, I received the greatest text of my life. It was a photo of Cornbread, Jimmy, and Jimmy's son, Max: three generations of Harris men together for a momentous occasion. Max, at twenty-one years old, had never met his grandfather before, and Jimmy hadn't seen his dad for what he thought might have been about thirty-five years. And in the middle, Cornbread, who had just turned ninety-four, had the glowing smile of a man who'd just won the lottery draw of a lifetime. Even on the small screen of my iPhone, the joy and relief captured in the photograph were radiant.

"Hey Andrea, hope you're good," Jimmy wrote. "Just a quick note of appreciation for connecting me with Chris. I was in town over the weekend to tape a segment for the Billboard Awards with Sounds of Blackness at Paisley Park. We filmed all day Sunday, but Monday as we were going to the airport Chris was able to coordinate a meeting to see my dad at his care facility. We spent some quality time together before I had to catch our flight. . . . He got to meet his grandson Max. . . . I'm back in LA now but Chris just texted me and said my dad was on Cloud 9 when he spoke to him today, so I just wanted to thank you."

I set down the screen and burst into tears.

In that moment, there was no question for me about what might happen next, or what I should do. In that moment, everything became quiet and clear, like the hush that falls over the city after the first winter snow. Later, Cornbread would tell me that this is when the angels brought me into his life. And you know what? After years of spending every Tuesday afternoon sitting with that tenderhearted, witty, wise man, I couldn't come up with an explanation that made any more sense than that.

"Isn't that what life is all about? Being able to help people along the way," Paul Peterson said when I talked to him about it all later. "At the end of the day, all we've got is each other."

BY THE SPRING OF 2022, as Cornbread and Jimmy were coming up on the one-year anniversary of their reunion and reconciliation, Cornbread started dropping more hints about how much he'd like Jimmy to join him onstage in Minneapolis. He spent much of their fifth Zoom call together preparing for that hopeful moment by teaching Jimmy the chords to his favorite compositions, using the call-and-response style to show him the structure of his songs "Blue Blue Blue Blues" and "Deeper Blues."

"We do really good if you play, I play, you play, I play. Okay?" he said, guiding Jimmy through the song. Turning to me, he said, "Okay, put the camera on the fingers on the piano," and I dutifully complied. With the iPad hovering overhead, Cornbread and Jimmy made their way through "Deeper Blues," each of them taking a turn playing a chord and a little bit of the melody. Before too long they ventured away from the main chorus of the song and into an evolving pattern of blues licks, with Jimmy listening intently for his dad's next cue. It was fascinating to watch them revert back to their teacher–student dynamic again, overcoming all the constraints of Zoom to play as if they were sitting side by side.

"Oh yeah," Cornbread said, looking up at the camera once they finished trading lines. "That's gonna be one of those where if you put it on the Internet, it'll go viral."

Riding high on the joy of their call-and-response collaboration, Cornbread made sure to mention his idea to Jimmy again: "I'm still trying to see if we can get together and have a big thing at the Hook and Ladder," he said. "I think we should put on a show that's national. And definitely Twin City-full. I think we should put on a show for the people."

"Right. Didn't we talk about that? I thought we were going to do that," Jimmy replied.

"Well, yeah! I'm still wanting to do it," Cornbread confirmed. "You remember!"

I gently interjected to remind them both that Cornbread was hoping this would happen for his ninety-fifth birthday concert, which was coming up in a couple of months.

"It's already on my calendar," Jimmy said, holding up his phone to the camera so we could see it. Sure enough, he had the whole day blocked off, with a note in all caps: CORNBREAD'S 95TH BIRTHDAY.

"Look at that. All day," Cornbread said, shaking his head. "Oh, it's gonna come to fruition! We're going to blow the roof off that place. Yeah, another memory thing in our lives, here."

"Yep," Jimmy agreed, smiling and nodding.

"Oh, man. I'm really looking forward to it. Two months," Cornbread said, counting the days on his hands. "And I promise I'm gonna live to be there! Ain't no stopping me now. And I can have the people that come to Palmer's, that always come and sit in—they'll all be there, and they'll be all blowing their heart out. It'll be the biggest thing the Twin Cities has ever seen!"

The next two months flew by in a giddy swirl of anticipation as Jimmy and Cornbread edged ever closer to playing in the same key, both figuratively and literally. For an early birthday present, and to make their online duets a little more harmonious, Jimmy offered to have Cornbread's piano professionally tuned. Under Cornbread's careful watch, the local musician and tuner Simon Husbands came to visit us one Tuesday afternoon and tenderly removed all of Cornbread's song books, statues, and trophies from the top of his upright piano, taking a photograph to make sure that he could put every item back exactly where it belonged. The following week, for their seventh Zoom call, Jimmy asked him how his newly tuned piano was working out.

"Everybody says it sounds better, but I was so used to hearing it sound bad that it kind of throws me a little bit," Cornbread replied, laughing. "But I can still do my thing," he added, launching into "Blue Blue Blue Blues" while Jimmy looked on and smiled.

"The funny thing about that is, that's what happens in life: you get used to something, which doesn't necessarily mean that it's the right thing: it just means that you're comfortable with it," Jimmy commented. "Everybody has their own perspective on things. So for you, it doesn't sound great because you were used to it the other way. To everybody else, it sounds great."

"You know, you sound like Cornbread's son," Cornbread responded, smiling proudly. "I mean, this wiseness, this smarts, this brain understanding—you got it going on, son."

"I got good training," Jimmy replied without missing a beat.

"Are we playing catch, here? What's the deal?" Cornbread said, delighted by the back and forth. "That's really true, really true. And nothing but the truth will set you free."

At the end of the call, Cornbread gave his son a homework assignment: since he'd taught Jimmy two of his songs, he wanted to know if Jimmy could send him two of *his* compositions for Cornbread to learn as well. The dream he'd described to me at our very first meeting was manifesting before our eyes.

The week of the show, I received a text from Jimmy: "In thinking about which song of mine I'd like to perform with Cornbread I'm thinking 'Human' makes sense," Jimmy wrote, including a link to the sheet music for the song he and Terry Lewis wrote and produced for the Human League in 1986. "It's popular and although it's based in romance the sentiment of forgiveness is present and appropriate under the circumstances."

The next day, I went to visit Cornbread and brought him the sheet music, the lyrics, and a recording of the song that we listened to together, with Jimmy joining in on Zoom.

So many nights I longed to hold you
So many times I looked and saw your face
Nothing could change the way I feel
No one else could ever take your place

I'm only human
Of flesh and blood, I'm made
Human
Born to make mistakes
(I am just a man) human

Please forgive me

The tears I cry aren't tears of pain
They're only to hide my guilt and shame
I forgive you, now I ask the same of you
While we were apart, I was human too

"We recorded that in Minneapolis, and it went Number 1. It was like a worldwide Number 1 record," Jimmy said on the call, clearly proud to belatedly share this success with his dad even though nearly thirty years had passed since it became a hit. "And the lyrics talk about how 'I'm only human, born to make mistakes.' And I just think that that's what we are. We're human."

"Wow. What a conclusion to come to. Very good, indeed," Cornbread said. "That's why I like talking to him," he said, turning to me. "It wouldn't really make no difference who he was; his genius thought that keeps popping into his brain, it comes out." He turned back to the screen. "I'm talking about you," he said, pointing at Jimmy.

"Thank you, that's nice. I appreciate that," Jimmy said.

"Ever since the day you walked into that daycare, man, I've been euphoric. You're just the most wonderfulest thing, outside of my other two children, of my life," Cornbread gushed.

"Thank you," Jimmy said, bowing his head.

After discussing a few logistics regarding the show, Jimmy signed off and Cornbread sat quietly at his piano, shaking his head. "Amazing call," he said. "Amazing, amazing. Like I keep telling Jimmy, I'm in a euphoric state, just beautiful. My life is just going so wonderful. I mean, I know it's selfish, but oh man, I'm just soaking it in. Come on with it, people! Come on."

"I don't think it's selfish," I said. "Everyone wants to celebrate you because you've got a big birthday."

He swiveled around on his bench to face his keyboard and started paging through his big book of old blues songs. "Here's a B-flat thing," he said, placing his hands on the keys and gently pressing down on a few minor chords. "I don't know my real name, don't know where I was born," he sang mournfully,

164

winding into the song "I've Been Treated Wrong" by Washboard Sam. "Don't know my real name, don't know where I was born. It seems like I was raised in an orphan's home. Well my mama died and left me—" he stopped, cutting himself off midline.

"My mama died and left me when I was only three years old," he said, turning to talk to me. "See how I go to reality from the song? How I made it this far, the Lord only knows," he said, finishing the verse. He shrugged and smiled. "I guess I got a right to be euphoric."

CORNBREAD'S NINETY-FIFTH BIRTHDAY PARTY was held at his beloved venue the Hook and Ladder in South Minneapolis on Friday, May 6, 2022. That morning, a big feature-length article about Cornbread ran on the front page of the Variety section of the *Star Tribune* and included quotations from Jimmy about his father's influence and their reconciliation, adding to the commotion around that night's festivities.

When I arrived at the Hook and Ladder that day, Cornbread's old pal Chris Mozena was running from one end of the venue to the other, tending to a film crew that Jimmy had hired to document the day and overseeing the staff who were setting up chairs and preparing for soundcheck. Once Cornbread arrived with his longtime drummer Doug Hill, Chris took him by the hand and helped him to slowly shuffle his way across the tented parking lot where he would perform that evening and head into the theater.

"There's going to be a lot of people here, Cornbread!" Chris said cheerfully. "This is going to be as many tickets as we've sold to any of your birthday parties."

Cornbread sat down in a chair and giggled, sipping from a Cornbread Special that the bartender mixed up for him and straightening his tie, which was decorated with black and white piano keys. After a few minutes, a hush fell over the room as all the members of the film crew started hustling around to get into position to capture Jimmy's entrance into the space.

PUT THE WORLD BACK TOGETHER

"We have a visitor," announced the filmmaker Joe Brandmeier, who had been tasked to capture the evening for posterity.

"A visitor from California?" Cornbread asked.

A heavy door swung open, and there he was. "Hey!" Jimmy said, sauntering toward Cornbread in his trademark black suit, fedora, and dark-rimmed glasses.

"Hey!" Cornbread said, looking him up and down. "You look just like your picture in the paper."

"I've got to look like myself, so you recognize me," Jimmy said, laughing and sitting down in a chair next to his dad. "How are you?"

"Very good. Very, very good," Cornbread replied, reaching out his hands to clasp Jimmy's in his own.

With cameras rolling and Joe tossing questions to them both, Cornbread and Jimmy quickly pivoted into performance mode, smiling into the crew's spotlights and reflecting on their relationship to one another and to music. Cornbread spent much of the interview clasping his hands together, giggling, and glancing over at Jimmy in awe, still adjusting to the fact that his long-estranged son was actually sitting beside him once again.

"I'm euphoric. That's my word. I'm sitting in the chair, right? But actually I'm floating around this room," Cornbread said. "I am so thankful. That's what God told me—be thankful—that I have a son that has made it in the world."

In a remarkable turn of events, it was announced just days before Cornbread's birthday party that Jimmy Jam and Terry Lewis would be inducted into the Rock and Roll Hall of Fame. They had been chosen for the category of Musical Excellence, meaning that their addition to the Hall came on the same day that the other inductees were announced rather than being included in an earlier round of nominees.

"Well, he was a great honor to me before anybody else thought about putting him in anything," Cornbread said, when asked about the announcement.

"I was in the son hall of fame?" Jimmy asked.

Father and son pause for a portrait in the midst of their much-anticipated reunion at the Hook and Ladder Theater in May 2022. Photograph by Nancy Bundt.

"Yeah, you were in *my* hall of fame," Cornbread said, nodding.

"That's the one that really matters," Jimmy said.

Before wrapping up the interview and starting their sound-check together, Jimmy took a moment to reflect on why he wanted to make the return home to share the stage with his dad that day. "The opportunity to be here was one that I couldn't pass up," he said. "For him to still be around at ninety-five, and not just around but living and vibrant and bringing blessings, as he says, into other people's lives and making them feel better—I wanted to be a part of that and just to see, in person, and watch him do what he does, which is make people feel good through his music."

Once Cornbread and Jimmy got up onstage for soundcheck with the rest of Cornbread's live band, it was clear that the elder Harris had no interest in figuring out a set list or planning out any of the night's details. Instead, he was going to spend every second relishing the fact that he and Jimmy were seated behind two neighboring keyboards and listening to each other play.

They ran through Cornbread's favorite tunes, including "Deeper Blues" and "Blue Blue Blue Blues," and Jimmy's relaxed, confident playing indicated that he had worked up some special licks to complement each song's key. Still, it was interesting watching him tamp down his own playing so that it fit behind whatever Cornbread was doing in any given moment; with Jimmy carefully, quietly waiting for cues, it was easy to imagine them in their original roles as the respected bandleader father and aspiring young musical son playing together all those years ago in Huckleberry Finn, Cornbread and Friends.

Backstage before the show, neither of the musicians seemed eager to leave the other's side. They sat for portraits together, made small talk with the band together, and each beamed proudly as someone brought Cornbread a copy of his feature in the *Star Tribune* and he asked me to read it out loud for them both.

For the first set that night, Jimmy came out into the audience and sat beside me to watch his dad play, smiling proudly and taking videos on his phone as Cornbread led his band through

Cornbread and Jimmy reunited onstage with support from Cornbread's backing band, which included Jon Pederson on guitar, Scott Soule on bass, Doug Hill on drums, Dean Brewington and Glen Graham on saxophones, Jason Marks on trumpet, and Nate Berry on trombone. Photograph by Nate Ryan.

many of his favorite standards, including "Blue Moon" and "In the Mood." Once he stepped onstage to join his dad for the second act, you could feel the energy in the room surge: the crowd pressed in closer to catch a glimpse of the celebrity producer returning home for a rare live performance, and Cornbread's band and horn players grew brighter and tighter, eager to impress the star in their midst.

Their performance got off to a funny start, as Cornbread had forgotten to turn his electric piano back on after the break. With a quick assist from Jimmy he was up and running, playing the opening chords of "Deeper Blues" alone and glancing over at Jimmy to join. You could hear a pin drop as the crowd awaited his son's accompaniment, and after a full spin through the song's chord changes, there it was: the gentlest tap of each chord coming from Jimmy's Roland synth, as if he were tiptoeing through the background of the song. The whole arrangement was so tender, with Dean Brewington adding a silky sax line over the top of Cornbread's playing, that it felt like easing into a warm bath. The audience, who had been dancing and bopping their way through the first set, spent the first song of Act Two holding very still and waiting to see what might happen next.

Things started to loosen up as Cornbread led the band into "The Cornbread Song," another tune he and Jimmy had played together over Zoom. As he set up the song ("The song got fairly famous," he explained. "A few people, I don't know, they must not like music or something: they decided they liked that song," he said, laughing), the band revved up behind him, and as soon as he sang the opening line Jimmy was ready to respond with a dizzying organ lick. It had been roughly fifty years since Cornbread had sat in with Jimmy's high school band Tanglefoot to play "The Cornbread Song" with the aspiring young musicians, but Jimmy easily fell into the song's cyclical rhythm and swinging choruses with the rest of the band.

Their third song together was an old standard, "Seems Like a Dream," which sent Jimmy back into tiptoe mode as he followed his dad's vocal melody and comping. When Cornbread sang the line, "Me and my baby had a falling out / I don't even remember what it was all about," he looked over at Jimmy and smiled, and the moment hit me like an arrow to the heart. At ninety-five, there wasn't much Cornbread *did* remember about why he and Jimmy drifted apart, and the whole time they were together indeed felt like a dream, or maybe the final scene in some dramatic movie. As the moment unfolded, Cornbread kept his composure and kept pressing on through the performance, spending more than an hour onstage with Jimmy as they wound through his favorite songs and the band grew more and more raucous. They did "Cool Rider" with Jimmy comping along and beaming, a delicate rendition of "Put the World Back Together" that had the whole crowd singing softly along, and an uproarious version of "When the Saints Go Marching In."

170

Watching Jimmy follow Cornbread's direction, it looked to me as if he had been transported back to the early '70s, when he was just a kid playing in his dad's band. It was like the past fifty years of his meteoric rise in the music industry had taken a back seat to his identity as Jim Harris's kid, the one whose dad taught him all those slick blues licks on the piano. Finally, after an hour onstage, Cornbread finally coaxed Jimmy to let it rip, and he took a lengthy, fiery solo as the crowd roared its approval. The kid could play!

The night's highlight came at the very end of the set, after the crowd spontaneously broke into a round of "Happy Birthday, Dear Cornbread," and the band seemed like it was about ready to pack up and leave the stage. Rather than say goodnight, Cornbread just kept on playing, wandering around his keyboard in search of another melody. Jimmy joined in, echoing his dad's lines, and creating a call-and-response like the ones they loved whipping up on their Zoom calls. The rest of the band lowered their instruments, the crowd hushed into silence again, and all three hundred of us seated under the tent that night listened to Cornbread speak to his son. Jimmy responded in kind with careful, loving melodies. When I glanced around the space, everyone around me was wiping away tears—including Jon Clifford of HiFi Hair, one of the punk rock angels whose impassioned letter to Jimmy helped nudge him closer to contacting his dad the year prior.

The band never did get around to playing Jimmy's song "Human," and a large white keytar that he'd arranged to have onstage for that moment remained in waiting, never touched by him or anyone else but gleaming brightly under the spotlights all the same. In hindsight, it would have been totally superfluous; everything that needed to be said had already been expressed through their musical conversation, and everyone who witnessed the exchange left with a deeper understanding of them both.

After the performance, Cornbread and Jimmy sat next to each other onstage for well over another hour, greeting each guest who

Cornbread Harris and Jimmy Jam Harris shared the stage for the first time in nearly fifty years on May 6, 2022, at the Hook and Ladder Theater. They reunited for Cornbread's ninety-fifth birthday party and had never played keyboards onstage together before. Photographs by Nate Ryan.

lined up to meet them, posing for photos, signing autographs, and hunching over Cornbread's piano keys together to play, joke, and laugh. It reminded me of what Jimmy had shared with me all those months ago when I first interviewed him about his dad, about how their patience and generosity with their fans was one of the things he knew they had in common even though they'd spent all those years apart. By the time Cornbread finally stood up from his keyboard, there wasn't a single person left in the audience, and it was well after midnight by the time Jimmy slowly, patiently helped him shuffle backstage.

It must have been after 2:00 in the morning by the time Cornbread and Jimmy finally left the venue. Despite the late hour, Cornbread's energy never waned, and he only appeared to get more and more alert as his time with Jimmy continued. Before leaving that night, Jimmy was sure to pack up a copy of Cornbread's article from the paper and leave his dad with a final birthday gift: his black Jam and Lewis baseball hat—the same one he wore every time we connected over Zoom, and which Cornbread always commented on during our calls.

Cornbread immediately put the hat on and beamed. "This thing's never coming off," he declared, sitting up straight in his chair and puffing out his chest.

After a long Minnesota goodbye, in which we all told each other thank you and good night at least a half-dozen times, I finally pried myself away from the Harris men and made my way home. Both Cornbread and Jimmy smiled at me as I walked away and kept waving until I rounded the corner of the green room door and headed out into the warm spring night.

Chapter 9

NEVER-ENDING LOVE SONG

The song will end, but the love keeps going out.

    —Cornbread Harris

Cornbread and I liked to joke about how hard it was going to be to wrap up a book about his life, because so much seemed to be unfolding well into his ninety-fifth year. Early on in our meetings together, he advised me not to rush through the process. "That's why I say, let it be a little longer to get the book written, because things are happening to me right now!" And that was before we'd ever done a single call with Jimmy or imagined that he'd become so involved again in his dad's life.

As we both marveled at the new developments that cropped up each week, Cornbread would shake his head in awe. "God is saying, 'Just wait! Just wait! You think you're blessed now?'"

"Hold on, it's about to get worse," I would often interject, finishing his thought in a way that I knew would make him laugh.

"It's going to get worse! That's right, that's right," he would respond, clapping his hands with delight.

In the two years that Cornbread and I worked the most intensely together on this book, it was really quite something to have a front-row seat to all that was going on in his life. In this period he was playing out more regularly than most local bands full of twenty- and thirty-year-olds, restarting his beloved weekly gig at Palmer's, and holding down two monthly brunch gigs at

Icehouse and Hell's Kitchen. He was also cast as an extra in a feature film, *Marmalade*, which starred *Stranger Things* actor Joe Keery and happened to be filmed in the small town of Jordan, Minnesota; and his song "Put the World Back Together" was licensed for the award-winning KARE-11 documentary *Love Them First: Lessons from Lucy Laney Elementary,* which followed the principal and students at a struggling North Minneapolis school over the course of a year.

Cornbread did all this while still teaching piano lessons to a whole family of siblings one night a week, receiving phone calls and doling out advice to his friends and members of his church congregation, and shuffling off to the bank once a month with his bass-playing friend Scott Soule to meticulously track his gig payments and make sure each member of his band received their fair share of his payouts and tips.

One week during our visit, Cornbread pulled out his old leather bank bag and unzipped it to show me how he tracked all his gigs. Inside were at least forty separate envelopes, each labeled with a musician's name and marked up with the dates they'd shared a stage with him and their percentage of the night's earnings. Anytime a new member joined his group or even just stopped by a gig to sit in, Cornbread would add a fresh envelope to the bag. The day he showed me this old-school cash accounting system, he'd just labeled an envelope with Jimmy's name and had a few hundred dollars' worth of cover charge and tips from the Hook and Ladder show waiting inside to be given to his son—an equal share of the night's proceeds that he had split between all eight musicians who joined him onstage.

Everything relaxed between Cornbread and Jimmy after they'd shared the stage at the birthday show. A few weeks after Jimmy had returned home to Los Angeles, we got on a call and saw that he was on a rare vacation. Rather than have to scramble off to another meeting or recording session, he had the entire afternoon free to lounge around a beachfront property that he had rented for the week and enjoy a long conversation with his dad. With

Father and son wear matching Jam and Lewis ballcaps while connecting for one of their many Zoom calls. Courtesy of the author.

Cornbread proudly wearing his newly acquired Jam and Lewis hat and Jimmy donning a matching one of his own, the two of them spent the first half-hour of the call raving about how fun it was to play together again.

"I'm mumbling a few words here and there because I'm speechless," Cornbread said, shaking his head. "I'm more or less forcing myself to talk. Because all I can do is keep repeating how wonderful it was. I still can't believe it. The music was like coming out of heaven. It was just coming out from the universe and lodging itself right there in the room with us. I mean, how do you explain something like that?"

"First of all, you couldn't really write this story in a believable way," Jimmy added. "People would go, no, that couldn't have happened. God's script, man."

"Amen," Cornbread said. "God's got it going on."

Anytime Cornbread ran out of things to talk about, he would quickly scan around the room to find something else he could do to fill the time and keep the call with Jimmy going. At one point, he got on the subject of his new walker and stood up from his piano to go retrieve it from the other room, then had me pick up the iPad and follow him around the narrow hallways of his house as he tried to squeeze it past the furniture and pick up some speed.

"Very fancy," Jimmy said, delighted by the impromptu demonstration.

As we stretched into our second hour together, Jimmy and I both had to plug in our respective devices to keep the batteries from draining, and he stretched out on the bed of his rental property, his face relaxed into a peaceful smile as he regaled us with stories about his kids and his recent attendance at a surprise birthday party for his longtime collaborator Janet Jackson.

"Did you say hello from The Cornbread?" his dad asked.

"Yeah, I did," Jimmy said, much to Cornbread's surprise. "I told her a couple weeks back that I'd been to play with you. She was happy. Everybody was happy—I told everybody."

"You're going around just blabbing, huh?"

"Yeah, I was blabbing. I told Bruno Mars when I saw him, and Anderson .Paak when I saw him, and Mary J. Blige when I saw her."

"I guess I'm doing the same thing," Cornbread added. "To everybody: I played with my son! I played with my son!"

Another half-hour went by, and neither Cornbread nor Jimmy wanted to wind down the call, so Cornbread was on the move again. This time he hopped up and went to "his office," which was actually the bathroom off his bedroom, to grab an old-school red leather-bound encyclopedia and bring it back to the dining room to show it to us both.

"That's my Google," Cornbread said, tapping the cover of the book. "They've got everything in here. The preamble to the Constitution, it just goes on and on and on."

He handed me the book and asked me to pull up something interesting to read. I flipped to the thesaurus section and found the word *Blessed,* and Cornbread egged me on as I read the definition out loud.

"Made holy, worthy of deep reverence—"

"Oh, I'm worthy of deep reverence! You are too," he said, beaming.

I continued. "Beatified by the Pope—"

"Oh, the Pope even thinks so," he enthused.

"—characterized by happiness, and bringing great happiness," I finished. "I think that's the right word for you."

"Oh yeah, that's it."

As Jimmy quietly smiled and watched his dad, Cornbread flipped around to talk about the various maps and reference guides—anything to make the call stretch on longer and to spend more of this uninterrupted time with his son.

Eventually, as our call neared the two-hour mark, Cornbread relented. "Well, James," he said, "other than this silly talk and I love you, I don't have too much else to say."

"Well, silly talk and I love you is perfectly sufficient," Jimmy responded, smiling.

"All right, now. Be very good to you and yours and yourself," Cornbread said.

"You do the same, sir. Have a great evening," Jimmy said, signing off.

Even after we hung up the call, it was one of those evenings when Cornbread didn't seem to want me to leave. He spent a little more time flipping through the encyclopedia, asking me to help him find Malibu on one of the maps so he could see just where Jimmy was spending his staycation with his family.

Before I left, Cornbread brought up something that I'd never heard him talk about before. He remembered back to a distant memory of when he cleaned houses and worked for a man who was blind and told me that he had started practicing in recent years for the day he suspected his own vision would fail him once and for all.

"I'm getting all ready. If the sight goes, I'll be able to still make it," he shared. "I'm learning how to play piano in the dark, so when I won't be able to see, I'll still be able to play. Like I say, God works in mysterious ways—he's given me time to get myself together to be able to do it."

Cornbread remained so focused on all of his many blessings in life that it was rare to hear him speak so candidly about the harder parts about getting older and knowing he was losing his once razor-sharp faculties. He certainly didn't dwell on it and changed the subject to something else quickly, but in that moment, with the encyclopedia open on the table between us, I was grateful that he was still finding ways to share new things with me after all this time we'd spent together.

ABOUT TWO MONTHS after Cornbread's big birthday show, I happened to have another trip to Los Angeles planned, and Cornbread tasked me with hand-delivering his envelope full of gig money to Jimmy. After showing the envelope to Jimmy on Zoom one day, I hopped a plane with it tucked carefully inside my bag and made my way to Flyte Tyme to visit him once again.

Seated in front of the stacks of keyboards and synthesizers in his private recording space at Flyte Tyme, I presented Jimmy with the money and a printed portrait of him with his dad at the Hook and Ladder show. As soon as he glanced down at the photograph, his memories of that reunion show came flooding back.

"In looking at this picture, it just looks like pure joy," he said.

"Both of you seemed like you were floating," I added.

"Yeah, we definitely were. And I know going into it, I didn't have any expectations. I tried not to think about it in my mind, like, what I thought it was going to be like, or what I thought I was going to feel or any of that stuff. I just experienced it. And it felt almost like a blink of the eye, and it was done," he said.

It was clear that I'd caught Jimmy in a reflective moment that day, and the more he spoke, the more introspective he became. "It just felt like a weight was lifted off his shoulders," he observed. "Whatever the weight of any guilt, or any—I don't know, whatever your feelings are, when stuff doesn't go the way you think it should go. And you've been carrying that around for so many years, in some way. And I just felt like all of that was—that was all done. You know? And in my mind, it was already done. But that was the physical manifestation of it. It was done."

For his dad's ninety-sixth birthday on April 23, 2023, Jimmy showed up at Palmer's Bar to pay Cornbread a surprise visit and watch him perform. Courtesy of the author.

I told Jimmy that I found it striking that he was so reticent to play over his dad at the gig, and that he didn't solo until his dad explicitly asked. Did he feel like he didn't want to steal the spotlight?

"I felt like I was just an accompanying player. I wasn't coming in to be the star," he said. "I was observing as much as I was playing. And I also enjoyed it because we never sat and played keyboards. Back in the day, it was me on the drums and him on the keyboards. So for me and him to be on keyboards together, that's the first time that's ever happened at a gig. So that made it even more special."

"That's how you talk to each other," I noted.

"Yeah. That's totally what it was," he said. "It was a musical conversation. And just, you know, the whole story, and all the things it took to get to that point."

I told Jimmy how it felt to watch them play the song "Seems Like a Dream" together, and how Cornbread seemed to sing the line "I don't even remember what it was all about" directly to him.

How remarkable, I said, that they were both able to change their feelings about the past without having to reopen every wound—a relitigation that might not even be possible for Cornbread this late in life.

"I didn't feel like there was any sort of explanation necessary," Jimmy concluded. "I didn't feel he owed that to me. You know, decisions were made. And I can either agree with them or not agree with them, whatever. It's all water under the bridge. So it doesn't really matter. I did okay, my kids are okay. He's okay. We're all okay. So let's just go from that point. And I also felt like I'm a product, really, of the two of them, and the fact that my mom let me drop out of school to pursue music is directly because of him. It's directly because she didn't let him, you know, take a leave of absence from his job to pursue music. And I never thought of that until maybe the last year, year and a half."

"And even their disagreements about things and the fact that, you know, he at one point just left—I get it," he continued. "Whether I agree with it, or whether that's the decision I would have made—but I totally get it. All of that was part of the way things turned out, you know. So I just have a different viewpoint about it now. And I'm just thankful about it. It all worked out the way it was supposed to."

As Jimmy spoke, I couldn't help but hear Cornbread's own voice and steady mantras (*"All of the hardships in my life turned out to be blessings"*) ringing in my ear. Everything Jimmy had shared with me at our very first meeting was true: they really were remarkably alike and were even reaching the same grand conclusions about their journeys through life. Despite their decades of separation, it turns out they had each been soaring along the same flight path.

CORNBREAD AND I spent a lot of our time together listening to music—and not only the songs that he felt inspired to play for me on the piano during our conversations, but recorded music that he would request that I play so we could hear it together. As he was riding high on the thrill of being connected with Jimmy again, Cornbread started talking about his love for the song "Nature Boy," written by eden ahbez and first recorded by Nat King Cole in the late 1940s. He brought it up unprompted one day, reciting each line of the lyrics word for word. Soon I was on Spotify pulling up the many different versions, and we listened to both Cole's version and a spare, emotional rendition by Ella Fitzgerald.

"The greatest thing you'll ever, ever learn," he said, repeating the song's chorus and sinking his weight into each word, "is just to love and to accept love in return."

He leaned back on his piano bench and thought for a moment. "You can be so smart—you can be a writer, you can be a waitress, you can be a great psychiatrist, or great scientist. But if you didn't learn to love and accept love in return, you missed a whole lot of life," he concluded.

"How does it feel now," I wondered, "to hear Jimmy tell you that he loves you after all these years? He says it at the end of every call."

"Oh yeah. I love you. Boy. You love me and you didn't speak to me for twenty-four years? No, stop, stop, stop," he said, cutting himself off and waving away his old resentments with a laugh. "Say thank you. I love you, too. That's it. Don't keep harboring that crap stuff. Shove the crap stuff away and take the good stuff in, and you'll just feel better, and work better, and look better. And then the people around you will feel better, too."

"It radiates," I said.

"It definitely does," he agreed, nodding.

Around the time we started listening to "Nature Boy" together, I got to thinking about Cornbread's legacy. It was not something he seemed to care much about; anytime I brought up the question of how he'd like to be remembered, he would shake his head and remind me that his only concern was being "accepted into God's eternity," and that he had no desire to dwell on what might happen here on Earth after he departed.

Still, as we dug further into his life story and especially as we made it through the end of one century's worth of memories and into the next, I couldn't help but think about all the people I'd talked to about Cornbread and how they described his impact on their lives. Overwhelmingly, and almost universally, all of the people who enjoyed watching Cornbread perform came away with the same impression of the experience: that he had an uncanny ability to lift people's moods, and to make them feel lighter and happier at the end of the night than they did when they first walked through the door.

Cornbread may not have had the opportunity to play a huge music venue or have his songwriting reach the masses through radio airplay or big album sales, but over the course of eight decades of continuous gigging he likely played hundreds of venues and entertained tens of thousands of people. The fact that he did it one small, intimate room at a time meant that most everyone who ever saw him play came away feeling like they had a chance to connect with him personally.

After a lifetime of granting requests, chatting up fans during intermissions and load-outs, telling stories between songs, and creating the soundtrack to people's weddings, happy hours, reunions, birthdays, fundraisers, and other life moments big and small, Cornbread had amassed a sprawling, organic network of fans who were eager to support him and come back to see him again and again. Whether he cared to think about it or not, I became convinced that his legacy was not unlike the chorus of "Nature Boy." He spent his life giving out love, and in his final years he had found a way to accept that love in return.

"I had to teach him, literally, how to say 'I love you,'" Cornbread's daughter Jennifer told me once, as she reflected on the ways her dad had changed over the years. "I used to say, 'I love you,' and he'd be like, 'Thank you.' Or he'd be like, 'You're welcome.' But now he says it. The other day, he's like, 'I love you. See? I said it!' Because he never heard it, you know?"

While attending the Minnesota Twins game on opening day in 2023 to watch Jimmy throw out the first pitch, Cornbread had the opportunity to meet his grandson Tyler Harris for the first time and reunite with grandson Max Harris and Jimmy. Courtesy of the author.

THE NIGHT BEFORE Jimmy's Rock and Roll Hall of Fame induction, I found him standing in the corner of a crowded West Hollywood dance club, surrounded by his wife and children, all of them dressed to the nines. As the deejay D-Nice kept the dance floor bouncing with Jam and Lewis–penned hits from The Time, Human League, Janet Jackson, and the Sounds of Blackness, Jimmy introduced me to his family and explained that I was the one on the other end of all those Zoom calls he'd been doing with his dad.

Jimmy had asked me to bring him a copy of the *Star Tribune*, which had just run a four-page spread on his and Terry's career in the Sunday paper, and he held up the front page of the Variety section and proudly showed it off to everyone around him. It was touching to watch him melt that way, stricken by the sight of his hometown paper giving him and his partner so much love, and he spent much of our short conversation at the club with his hand clasped to his chest, as if he were trying to physically hold himself together in the midst of a swirl of press interviews, parties, and special events leading up to the following day's ceremony.

Before I bid him adieu, I leaned in to give him the message that I promised I'd deliver from Cornbread. "Your dad wanted me to tell you congratulations, and that he loves you," I yelled into his ear, doing my best to project over the music. Whether he heard me or not, I cannot say, but I do know that he asked me to say it again. "Congratulations, and he loves you," I repeated, and Jimmy rocked back, closed his eyes, held his hand to his heart, and breathed it in.

"Thank you," he said softly, his voice barely breaking through the din. "Thank you."

WHEN CORNBREAD AND I talked to Jimmy, the younger Harris would often break out into mini soliloquies about the things he'd learned about human nature, and one idea he returned to in our calls was how he believed that over time people forgot most of the details about who said what, or who did what to whom in any given moment. Speaking to us over Zoom one day, Jimmy noted, "People don't remember the details of stuff. But what they do remember is how you made them feel."

"Amen, you nailed that one," Cornbread responded. "I think you might have said that before once or twice, but that's okay," he added, laughing.

"You can repeat your hits," Jimmy joked.

"Yep," Cornbread agreed. "Like I say, put it at the beginning of the book, put it at the end of the book. Keep repeating that good stuff."

As I reflected more on what Jimmy said, I recognized just how remarkable it was that for decades all that existed for both of them was how the other one had made them feel. But now, right in front of my eyes, they had somehow arrived at a place where they were able to change that feeling. Much like a jazz chord progression might build up tension across several bars of a song before resolving into a more serene major chord, the end of Cornbread's song brought him back to the root note and rang out in a clear, bright harmony.

When I first heard Cornbread sing "Deeper Blues," I got hung up on the heartache of the lyrics and bitter feelings of resentment expressed by the song's protagonist. In our later days together, as I listened to him playing it alone at his piano, I saw that the way Cornbread composed the song actually expressed an undeniable feeling of hope: that no matter how painfully life might twist and turn us, there is always another opportunity to break into a joyful chorus and end in a major key.

One of my favorite Cornbread songs is an original instrumental composition that he titled "Never-Ending Love Song." It has a serene, meditative quality, especially when he performs it alone; it sounds like it could be a long-lost Vince Guaraldi track for one of the Charlie Brown movies, or maybe the score to a short film about finding a river to skate away on.

When I asked him where the melody came from, Cornbread shrugged and said, "I'm confused about that one myself. It's something that kept going through my mind, it kept getting stuck in there. So I said okay, I'll give it a title." He turned around on his bench and floated away, gently hammering on a single note and then fluttering around to the rest of the melody's swirling notes. "My band said, 'What are you going to call that?' And I said, 'Never-Ending Love Song.'"

"So you don't know where it started or where it ends," I observed.

"That's right. It's something that just came into my brain and there it was. And such continuity! I mean, actually a nice chorus topline, you know? I never heard anything exactly like that. So

Cornbread gets lost in a song while having his photograph taken at the Hook and Ladder Theater in the fall of 2021. Photograph by Nancy Bundt.

there it was. So I play the song, and I tell the people, I say, 'Well, the song has ended, but the love is still going out.'"

What better way to summarize my time spent with this remarkable artist and man? Of course the song didn't end that day; he was so energized by talking about the composition that he had to place his hands back over the piano keys and stir up the melody for another go-round. As I sat there listening, I had the same feeling that I experienced the very first time I watched him play in the studio, and every time I went to see him at Palmer's, and all the other times I'd seen him wander his way around those keys. For the beautiful, fleeting moment that existed inside that song, there was only Cornbread and his piano, one man communing with his muse, channeling all of the hardships and triumphs of his long life into a beautiful melody and gathering every last bit of his strength to send all the love from his fingertips out into the spectacular, blessed universe.

AFTERWORD
JIMMY JAM

Over the past few years I've had the chance to think a lot about my philosophy of success. I have concluded that being successful is simply doing what you want to do in life. The same summer that I reconnected with my dad, Terry and I released our first album as recording artists, *Jam and Lewis, Volume 1*. When it debuted at Number 1 on iTunes, somebody said to me, "Man, that's great. You've got a Number 1 album." And I said, "No, what's great is that we even made an album." Quite honestly. I mean, people liking or not liking it is part of it. But the success for us was just getting it out. The fact that it even exists is a success. I remember always saying to the artists we've produced over the years to remember the success of finishing. No matter what happens from this point, hit record or not, the success is in just getting it done, so be pleased with that.

When I think of success in relationship to my dad, I think his success is enjoying the opportunity to make music. And at ninety-seven years young, I believe it's the music that keeps him young. Whether you've made it to the top of the charts or sold millions of records—that, to me, is more other people's measure of success. But I think doing what you love to do? That is the ultimate success. And I know I feel that way because of the things Cornbread wasn't able to do when I was young, because he sacrificed his career to raise me so that I could have mine.

All these years later, I think that's maybe one of the things that still drives him. He's not trying to have any sort of success on the charts or anything like that. He knows that just being able to do music is successful. And he's doing exactly what he loves to do: changing the lives of all the people who come to see him perform.

I admire that about him. I admire a lot of things about him. I know that I'm the person I am because of him.

When I asked my dad what he wanted for his ninety-fifth birthday, he said he didn't want presents but wanted my "presence" at his birthday gig in Minneapolis. It was truly a gift I couldn't have imagined. We hadn't played together for nearly fifty years, so the chance to sit down and have a long musical conversation with him was, in his words, "euphoric." I documented this once-in-a-lifetime event and shared the video with him as a Father's Day gift and also shared it with a few close friends I thought would understand.

One of my friends called me and said, "Hey, I loved when you sent me that tape of your dad." He and his dad are estranged. He said, "Now I know where you get your funk from." Because hearing Cornbread play, he could hear where I get my stuff from. And I said, "Yeah, that's because that's where I learned to play." It was cool that he noticed that.

I ended up sending the video of our reunion to about twenty people who I thought would get it, and they all got it on levels that I didn't even expect. People who were estranged from their fathers said, "I'm going to go back home now and do it." Other people had the feeling of regret that they never got that chance. People had a range of emotions, but everybody could see the joy. They could see it. And that's what was really cool.

My dad has a song called "Put the World Back Together." For that to happen, it needs to start one relationship at a time. I hope our coming back together after almost half a century apart sets an example of hope and healing, and inspires the world.

ACKNOWLEDGMENTS

This book simply would not exist were it not for the willingness and kindness of Cornbread Harris, who welcomed me into his dining room every Tuesday for more than two years to embark on this journey with him. It was the thrill of a lifetime to sit just a few feet from him while he serenaded me on the piano, which he did at least once or twice every time I visited. All told, we recorded ninety-six interviews together, which is also the same age he was when I wrapped up the first draft of this book. When I shared this fact with him, he said, "You're hooked into the universe, kid."

Likewise, this project was deeply enriched by the participation of Jimmy Jam, who welcomed me into his world with warmth and shared his memories generously. Cornbread, Jimmy, and I connected over Zoom for twenty-seven separate on-the-record interviews (which gradually morphed into hangout sessions, and then opportunities for both of them to hear me read this book to them out loud), plus a handful of in-person interviews and special events that I will cherish forever.

I would also like to give a special thank-you to Cornbread's wife of thirty years, Sabreen Hasan, and to his daughter, Jennifer Harris, for their ongoing support of this endeavor, and for granting me entrance into his home and access to his photo albums, scrapbooks, and memorabilia. Thank you as well to Cornbread's longtime bandmates, especially Scott Soule and Doug Hill, who helped me to understand his legacy as a bandleader.

In addition to Cornbread's own personal collection of artifacts, I also called on many publicly available resources to flesh out the backstory of his family and remarkable career. I've lost track of just how many hours were spent combing the online newspaper archives now hosted by the Minnesota Historical Society (what an incredible resource!), which is where I found early clippings mentioning Cornbread's grandparents and parents in the Black community newspapers the *St. Paul Echo* and the *Northwestern Bulletin Appeal,* and mentions of Cornbread, his many bands, his former wife Bertha Harris, and a young Jimmy Harris in the *Minneapolis Spokesman-Recorder.* I also found numerous clippings mentioning Cornbread and his previous bands in the *Minneapolis Star* and *Tribune* archives housed at newspapers.com.

I would also like to thank the patient librarians (shout-out to librarians!) at the Minneapolis Central Library's Special Collections, the Minnesota Historical Society's Gale Family Library, and the University of Minnesota's Andersen Library for accommodating my many very specific requests, especially in the midst of a pandemic when in-person visits to view artifacts required extra layers of protection for us all.

Finally, I'd like to offer an extra special thank-you to copy editor Louisa Castner, the crew at the University of Minnesota Press, and to my eternally patient editor, Erik Anderson. This project came as a surprise to us both, and I am so grateful that he immediately wholeheartedly agreed to support it through all its unexpected twists and turns. Erik, you are now one of Cornbread's punk rock angels. It's an honor and you wear it well.

CORNBREAD'S DISCOGRAPHY

SOLO ALBUMS

Cornbread Harris, *Live at Nikki's* (1996)

Cornbread Harris and Friends, *Cornbread Supreme, Volume I* (2002)

Cornbread Harris and Friends, *Cornbread Supreme, Volume II* (2002)

Cornbread and Friends, *Live at the Hook & Ladder, Volume 1* (2018)

Cornbread and Friends, *Live at the Hook & Ladder, Volume 2* (2019)

James Samuel "Cornbread" Harris Sr., *The Creation Session* (2021)

COLLABORATIONS

Augie Garcia Quintet, "Hi Ho Silver" b/w "Going to Chicago" (1955)

Augie Garcia Quintet, "Drinking Wine Spoli Oli" b/w "Hello Baby" (1955)

James Bonner, "Don't Rush It" b/w "Stumpin'" (1971)

Cadillac Kolstad & The Flatts vs. Cornbread Harris, *All the Fun (At Palmer's Bar)* (2010)

Jack Klatt & The Cat Swingers, *Mississippi Roll* (2012)

INDEX

ANDREA SWENSSON is an author, podcast host, and music journalist in Minneapolis. She hosts the Official Prince Podcast and has contributed music journalism to NPR Music, *Pitchfork, City Pages,* and Minnesota Public Radio's The Current, where she previously hosted The Local Show. Her book *Got to Be Something Here: The Rise of the Minneapolis Sound* was published by the University of Minnesota Press and received a Minnesota Book Award.

JAMES "JIMMY JAM" HARRIS III, the son of Minnesota blues legend James "Cornbread" Harris, is a Grammy-winning songwriter and producer from Minneapolis. He and Terry Lewis, known as Jam and Lewis, were inducted into the Rock and Roll Hall of Fame in 2022.